Trevor Dannatt: buildings and interiors 1951/72

Lund Humphries London/Crane, Russak & Company Inc. New York

Copyright © 1972 by Trevor Dannatt
First published 1972 in Great Britain by
Lund Humphries Publishers Limited
12 Bedford Square, London WC1

Paperback   SBN 85331 339 3
Clothbound SBN 85331 345 8

Published in the United States by
Crane, Russak & Company, Inc.
52 Vanderbilt Avenue, New York, NY 10017

Library of Congress catalog no. 72-83714
ISBN 0-8448-0066-X

Designed and produced by
Pentagram Design Partnership

Printed in Switzerland by
Buchdruckerei Berichthaus, Zurich

roduction

rs is a society rich in irony: swinging London the
tal of a vanished empire, a Socialist state run
Capitalist principles, mining companies prospect-
our National Parks, the world's largest con-
tration of architects presiding over the
cifixion of our cities. We have made vast invest-
ts in railways and then closed the stations,
oads which have scarified the towns, in rockets
: won't lift and aircraft which no one wants

this paradoxical situation there are, naturally,
any responses as there are individuals. In
eral architects are so caught in the mechanism
uilding, so much part of the intricate system
nance and technology that they are aware of
a vague unease. Everything is so obviously for
best, yet somehow the outcome is quite other

well-intentioned world it is difficult to find
apegoat, and the public has recently shown
ndency to blame the architect. Yet, probably,
er was there a better-intentioned professional
up of men. They have bent in all directions to
ot themselves to the requirements of the modern
ld. They have embraced technology, management,
control, computer programming, regional
ning, sociology, even, in extreme cases (not
essarily with reluctance), politics

as been a mammoth effort in re-education, mind-
tching on a vast scale. The architect of today
aybe a little disillusioned about the world,
still perfectly confident of his mental agility
his capacity to create on a large scale.
process of his education has brought him
urally to think in increasing magnitudes

resist this seemingly inevitable progression has
ved difficult as well as unprofitable. Successful
itects tend to become administrators and the
easing scale and tempo of modern life work
nst concentration on particular things. They
ss for blanket solutions. The architect has had
bsorb a huge quantity of new information.
he process an equally large body of expertise has
btrusively leaked away. What has largely gone
articular and unquantifiable information:
to qualify parts and make them significant,
n the scale of roofs and walls to the scale of
dows and doors. How to do specific things – for
mple, design fixings, hinges, handles, railings,

pavings… To provide appropriate accent, make
connections and telling junctions and corners.
Such information is difficult to transmit. It depends
on a continuous interaction with skilled men of all
kinds and this has quietly evaporated under the
impact of linear technology

The traditional process of design, by observation,
by imitation and by development, has been eroded
by the compulsion to be continuously original and
by the decay of the crafts associated with building

Particular things are required only by particular
individuals. As clients become increasingly
impersonal, Boards and Committees dominated by
the fear of commercial failure and therefore by the
priestly accountant, particularity is not so much
excluded as unconsidered. No one would dare
propose an act of faith and the architect who does
so is careful to disguise his intentions

The kind of loving experience of form, space and
material that was once the architect's raison d'être
is obtainable today often only at the scale of
furniture and fittings, interiors and exhibitions.
Even here, each item tends to be pre-empted by a
specialist designer. For example, lighting becomes
a technical matter instead of a total experience

A few architects in the past twenty years have been
fortunate in working intensively at an almost
mediaeval scale, often directly with craftsmen, and
have been able to take their technology in relatively
small, immunizing doses. They have learnt to
handle intractable materials, like concrete and steel,
glass walls and industrial panels in small buildings
and have slowly brought an accumulation of
experience to bigger tasks

This process could be condensed before the twentieth
century by the mastery of relatively elementary
technologies – the nineteenth century had many
brilliant men – Pugin, Street, Scott, Mackintosh –
who produced major works before they were 30.
Today our most talented generation is over 40 and
only now beginning to practice on any scale. They
have come to modern architecture as a third
generation, students and assistants to the pioneers
of the movement in England (themselves followers
of the great European masters: Aalto, Le Corbusier,
Gropius, Mies van der Rohe). They were involved
with CIAM (Trevor Dannatt was the last secretary
of the MARS Group) and largely instrumental in

its dissolution. What a saga that was. It is with great
difficulty that one can imagine a worldwide, respectable and successful organization committing an
honourable suicide. In the world of Norman
Parkinson it is unbelievable

At first they accepted the dogmas of their elders,
but as the years passed, and the feedback began to
come in, they have become steadily more independent, dispersed and isolated. No longer a group,
they are none-the-less bound by a concern for building, to the thing itself, to the supremacy of
construction and detail and a concern for quality.
For all their occasional exercises in planning and
forays into theory, they are almost all committed
to the idea of the work of architecture, to the
building as a work of art, an unpredictable factor in
the environmental equation. They have therefore
become involved with history, with geometry and
proportional theory, with analysis of classic plans,
with looking and conserving, in short, with relearn-
ing the business of being an architect, a creator of
form and space, in the great and continuing tradition
of the art

They have, in effect, arrived at a traditional point
of view, across an enormous divide of theory and
practice. It is a view which has its problems, for
around us young intellectuals are destroying art
(yet again) and the world is moving into ever greater
crises of affluence and expectations. Technology
becomes ever more evanescent, concerned with
systems and not with products. The architect is
hardware oriented, all his history is involved with
objects and their making

It requires an effort of will to retain the sense of
quality, of the value of the building itself in the face
of economic and technological pressures. The value
of those who practice in this doggedly unfashionable
and largely unpatronized way is all the greater to the
society that respects but does not create
opportunities for them

Patronage was once the prerogative of princes.
Today an occasional minister can sway a commission
but the real power lies in the public and private
bureaucracies. Their inevitable choice is for the
large organization of proven mediocrity

Yet virtue does occasionally triumph: among others,
Colin Wilson has the British Museum extension,
Denys Lasdun is completing the National Theatre,

the Smithsons have built the Economist building. The generation has achieved some splendid and honourable buildings – and a remarkable number of professors

Trevor Dannatt has grown his practice slowly. He worked at first with Jane Drew, who is infinitely generous, enthusiastic and energizing, and Maxwell Fry, buoyant, humane and poetic. Through them he became involved in the editorship of the Architects' Year Book, which was to become a forum for architectural discussion and polemic in the fifties. In working on the Festival Hall he came in close contact with Leslie Martin and Peter Moro, whose influence has greatly affected his professional life and through whom he became involved in the MARS Group. Moro had been his tutor at the Polytechnic and his continental training, his planning skill and sardonic criticism had profoundly influenced a generation of students. Sir Leslie Martin has been instrumental in his obtaining some important university work and something of Martin's cool quality comes through in many of Dannatt's buildings

But the cool is largely his own, and it comes from a puritan, non-conformist background as much as anything. In the fifties, Dannatt, a friend of Finn Juhl, was much involved with Scandinavian design, especially Danish and Finnish, and he learned a great deal from it, a kind of craftsmanly elegance, a comfortable lightness of touch, which immunized him almost completely from the Brutalism that followed in the sixties

It is yet another of our contemporary ironies that one of our best architects should build his major work in the middle of the Arabian desert. The great hotel and conference centre at Riyadh was won in a limited international competition and is now nearing completion. The quality of the work is extraordinary and the complexity of the project is equally daunting. It is a monument in precisely the same way as the Foreign Office of Gilbert Scott; it pins down a moment of grandeur and creates an object which is considerably greater than the sum of its parts

There are three main buildings, a monumental conference hall and its associated rooms and foyers, extrovert and dominant; an hotel which looks in upon itself into tall balconied foyers, an interior landscape to set against the brown sun-glazed desert outside; and a mosque as open and simple as a non-conformist chapel, which takes up precisely the form of the local mosques and translates it simply into the twentieth century. It will be, God and politics willing, a notable achievement

In this anthology the reader will be able to see the growth of a sensibility, at first awkward, tentative but always tender and concerned. This sensibility has grown and become assured. Dannatt is not on the verge of a breakthrough. Such a concept is not in his nature, which is unassertive, patient, fastidious and persistent. But he is on his way

Theo Crosby

graphical

...n 1920, London
...cated Colfe's School and the School of
...chitecture, The Regent Street Polytechnic
...3–48, Office of Maxwell Fry and Jane Drew,
...efly with the late Bronek Katz
...8–51, Architect's Department, London County
...uncil, Festival Hall Group
...52, commenced private practice
...57–60, associated architect with Sir Leslie
...rtin for College Hall, Leicester and London
...niversity Precinct
...67, appointed architect for Riyadh Conference
...entre following international competition

...onorary secretary, MARS Group, 1952–57
...itor, Architects' Year Book 1948–62,
...lodern Architecture in Britain', Batsford, 1959

...ients include

...he Universities of Hull and of Leicester
...rinity Hall, Cambridge
...he Governors of Bootham School
...reater London Council
...nner London Education Authority
...ondon Boroughs of Lambeth and of Southwark
...he Friends Service Council
...he Council of Industrial Design
...ritish Transport Commission
...Walter Thompson Co. Ltd
...Government of the Kingdom of Saudi Arabia

...urrent work

...ootham School development plan
...ociety of Friends Meeting House, Blackheath
...ondon Borough of Lambeth, old people's home
...nd housing, Union Road, SW
...Albany' housing, Corm Estate, Beirut
...Greenwich Building Society, new offices
...Consultant, Brummana School, The Lebanon

Jury member for

CoID Design, Architectural Design Project, Civic
Trust and RIBA Regional Awards
Derby Civic Halls, Bristol Ashton Court and
Tangier Bay Development Competitions

'A plea for quality'

Transcript of a talk given at the Royal Institute
of British Architects, 21 January 1969, in the series
'Architects on Architecture'

These occasions seem to be ones where the personal
pronoun can be used without diffidence. For example,
'I believe' and 'I think this', 'I do this', seems a possible
structure for a talk. In fact, instead of methods,
what I have put down is, I think, about ideals and
duality of attitude: on one hand scepticism about the
march of progress, growth/development, production/
sales, in short our advertised architectural/social
programmes and methods; on the other hand the
wish to be employed at a certain scale, believing it is
right to occupy space and build in a certain, maybe
more personal, way, satisfying physical needs and
perhaps giving significance to them at another level.
So I have put together thoughts on problems that
interest or distress me, that I'm in a dialogue with
myself about, related to the conserve or develop
dichotomy, in the hope that the struggle to express
them may interest and not be too sententious!

Broadly, these talks have been personal testaments
by practising architects, combining generalized
views with straight professional opinion. Perhaps,
too much in the 'what makes me tick' category as
opposed to showing particular works in relation to
theory or speculative research. But the intention has
been 'the practitioner speaks'. We are GP's, not
working for the Wellcome Foundation, yet even so
we are not all in the same position and in general
these personal statements, despite the common
ground of involvement in building, have shown very
divergent attitudes, almost, you might say, ranging
from Benthamite to Wagnerian

It would be too easy to hang a talk on one's hates,
it is necessary to indicate one's loves (or sacred
objects) but can one show how one works, how,
let us say, philosophy informs day-to-day routine
and (since ours is a practical world as well) vice-
versa. This is not easy, for unless one is a political or
technical fanatic one's philosophy is semi-solid, one
hopes, developing, not an exact ideological statement
precept by precept. There is no one way to attain
grace but, naturally, if you are goal-oriented everything becomes easier and it is possible to be didactic,
a firm believer in this and that, doubts are out and
off we go – 'onward Christian soldiers'

In passing, I am amazed at the certainty with which
others speak about matters that to my mind can be

seen in at least two ways. Perhaps it is that I'm
unwilling to become polarized about what is marginal,
a condition which is now endemic in our architectural society. What often appear to be broad views
too often turn into narrow ones taking this or that
facet as the whole subject; as a panacea rather than
one of many tools to be used as we may to enhance
or enslave life

I start from love of buildings. Life passes quickly and
is often sharp or touched by bitterness. Literature
is consoling because it makes order, shows a whole
view of human life, sets it in a matrix. Likewise,
architecture. Thus through ancient or more recent
buildings we see an image of a whole society. Man in
an ecological situation, against ours where we seem
divorced from environment, not part of it – masters
of it and heaven help our room mates

From even a fragment of an old building we receive
intense satisfaction, a sense of the depth and continuity of life. You say that this is an extra-architectural
quality – just historico-romantic. I say no, for we
receive it too from a few of our contemporaries.
Against such standards how can we not be dissatisfied
with our own efforts, our short-term views of mini-
mal space and material, producing buildings without
sense of time or quality, not helping man to relate
to his environment but leaving him perched upon it,
ready to jump down and gobble up that which
attracts

Maybe one's working philosophy is muddled, thought
process whimsical, and knowledge often seems
acquired at random. This one is trying to correct
all one's life, nevertheless, at every moment one is
considering alternatives, selecting, rejecting, or
reserving judgement, not just on a taste basis. Saying yes or no, but also certainly, probably, possibly,
unlikely. Qualifying, not pontificating. Unless we shut
off, content with our given apparatus and prejudices
we are subject to a host of influences. Living and
working we build up inside us, with time, like a coral
reef, an architectural bedrock. Perhaps not the best
metaphor for coral is so much dead polyp. Perhaps
instead an inner architectural organism that is in
process of renewal, at the same time, one hopes,
changing, developing

I hope that this talk will amount to something more
than a string of accumulated aperçus, a self-justifi-
cation or self-advertisement, and that the mulling
over of a few years' work will show some personal
development that may have some modest general
significance. Perhaps in the sense that what I have

done in the way of building has grown out of problems and has not been imposed upon them – at least that was the intention

Speaking personally, until recently my commissions have been on the edge of things, perhaps special problems, or is it possible that every building is a special problem? Circumstances might lead me to think so. I can say we were faced with those requirements and situations and we did this. This seems a simple enough basis for explanation but... what a vast stretch lies between instruction and action. Of course, there is the line of least resistance – 'what did we do last time' – rather than reconsideration, speculation and heart-searching too, before decision and after. I believe one forges the equipment to deal with the next task in this way, strengthened by what has gone before. Each problem has its roots in previous ones but also drops seeds into future tasks

I said we are like GP's. Even so, we have to attend to what is called the development field, though perhaps theoretical studies is a more appropriate description of the sort of work that affects our way of regarding the context of building – what we have to relate back to while making here-and-now decisions. For instance, the Cambridge theoretical studies in land use show a new direction with profound urban and urbane implications. At another level, to me a lot of 'research' in building science (or is it scientism?) seems marginal and often only throws up wonder systems or materials: as it were, how many angels can dance on a preferred dimension

However, faced with a new problem, or the old one again, we turn to case histories, available data, to speculative research which we consider in the light of what we and others have done. Honourable and necessary, this is a critical part of our vocation. We don't work in a vacuum and originality, certainly in the novelty sense, is to be discouraged, though I think one condemnation in this series was too unqualified. We have to distinguish. Buildings can be outstanding, can be show-biz, can be reticent or mediocre. If you like, 'his building is original at all costs, your building is forward-looking, my building is seminal'

I think, perhaps, it would be more accurate to say that every building can be regarded as a stage in the development of the type and at the same time a special case, even though this may be a dubious biological metaphor

When first in practice, despite the satisfactions of work, small tasks sometimes seemed irrelevant in one's awareness of larger contexts. However, a belief sustained what one was doing. Gradually, tasks became larger and even though they might not be regarded as central problems I'm not unhappy about comparisons of scale of work or volume – though I'm dismayed by the idea of architecture as business, and the fallacy of size, the thought that we might solve our problems by making them bigger. Disproved to my mind, by what can be seen happening all around in the callous destruction of environment and the dichotomy between what is publicized and what actually is provided in built form

I hardly need say that in general the quality of our environment is worsening. For example, air travel is such a simple idea that we might expect the environs of an airport to have some relevant pattern, but despite progressive legislation and good intentions, most airport scenes show immense efforts at control and no corresponding significant order. We liked railways because they had just this. Termini, junctions, main stations, local stations, cuttings, tunnels, embankments, bridges, all spoke the same language. An ordered hierarchy of control, all fitted together. Even today the fragments show the relevant pattern. Clear, precise ordering of transport through the length and breadth of the country and a hierarchy of speed (train, horse carriage, bicycle, pedestrian)

Or, at another scale, in a hill town like say, Shrewsbury, delight has vanished over the years. The one-way streets produced by traffic schemes with endless flow and noise have destroyed what is lightly called amenity

So we all know that with the individualistic automobile total accessibility means total vulnerability and as professionals we have possible solutions, though we probably continue to enjoy door-to-door transport as long as we can. We each add our piece of destruction as in self-defence we drive on in our isolator with the illusion of a certain sort of freedom, while real liberty is slowly eroded. But how can we start to design without respect and a feeling for use?

This theme is too common and not constructive, after all, loss of amenity, impersonal scale are common complaints. In old cities, opportunities for redemption are lost for ever as we pull down, leaving perhaps a few five-starred buildings to be set in a conglomeration of wrong scale redevelopment. In Edinburgh and Dublin it's just starting. Important cities for they show fine architecture in a fine building context of appropriate characteristic scale. It's not only the monument but the matrix which is important. Just

at the tourist level it will soon be worth preser almost everything. Long live tourism!

At the level of, say, London, personally I'm more distressed at what continues to happen. The grad disappearance of meaningful relations between b ings: perhaps the old was not that wonderful bu had some sense of scale and possibility of humar sociability. In this field I have nothing to recomme only a certain scepticism about planning. For insta I wonder about the old height restriction code wh at least produced some sort of order, not the fra mentation into super-plots, which seems to follo comprehensive development. Amsterdam did it, a European life is enriched in consequence

When we go on holiday the chances are that we descend on countries where older patterns persi You may laugh at it, but a need is expressed whe developers in France actually build 'old' ports fo leisure life, glossily described as 'build your own picture postcards'. It seems we fail to make place significant for either work or leisure

If it's not the Costa Nova or the faceless city, we c enjoy the aspirations of an international exhibitio with its fatuous, but perhaps appropriate, technic exhibitionism and the architecture of show, whic unfortunately eventually spills over into real life

At Montreal, apart from some smaller nations, th national pavilions were as pompous as the ones I sav in Paris in 1937. A jumble of monuments with the meaningful order of a Christmas tree. There was little about the quality of life, lots about our egocen world view – 'man shall inherit the earth'. I'm surprised that a colleague should be surprised at one c the Montreal draws – a hand-carved model village. A queue of simple people to see something human, humble in the blatant world of conceit where technologism goes to bed with national socialism

A world so very different from what was imagined, say, when a student just pre-war, with our sort of faith in the international future (man blessed by technology and the care of the state). Experience has lighted dreams, for while social and technical factor seem useful points of departure, they do not now impress as solely contributing to happiness. Other factors have to be considered and I believe we shoulc aspire to relieve the anthill of society and technology rather than be the apostles of the brave new world. A world which physically, despite the efforts of our distinguished colleagues, consists more and more of

e vast developments of Mr X or Y or those
the-peg housing schemes of the Council of Z'

t does this add up to? Just a warning to practi-
ers to think again before action? Just the sense
ustration of those committed to a certain type of
tice in their middle years? Or the question,
we go on, without becoming too much of an
nization, fortunate in being able to make some-
g whole in a world where fewer and fewer are
to do so? Adding our bit to the environment,
aps hoping to release the potentialities of a
ation or develop a milieu that may produce inter-
n and even some pleasure. Content, I hope, to
fewer materials while trying to do well, even
n it may soon be engulfed in a megadevelopment

asionally it's difficult not to have a sneaking
rd for size and power, even while deploring it.
n one wonders, in the context of a growth-
ntated society, has the smaller firm any validity
it grows at all can it do well and escape the fate
seems to overtake once-admired practices?
r Raymond Aron's sympathetic view:

hose sectors where there is no imperative need
giant firms, the reliance placed upon individual
tures, in the domain of the numerous services
endered or permitted by rising levels of living,
ot only rational in the economic sense, but is
spensable to preserve the diversity of human
tionships and to provide opportunities for those
o wish not to make a career in administration,
to work on their own account, in short, to main-
an adequate independence of society from the
e'[1]

esutti spoke well when he said that the architect's
is to be 'the leader of a profound love of quality'.
n't think this means preferring marble to PVC
, apart from secondary things, implies caring
ply about order, about the structuring of environ-
t at a moment when fragmentation through
cialisation increases and buildings, spaces, second-
and tertiary objects no longer fit together but
their own separate ways

course, we have to work at the level at which we
employed, but pay regard to lesser and greater
gnitudes of scale. Search for the general in the
ticular and particularize the general. We should
to clarify the nature of our tasks and determine
importance as well as the relative value of its
ponents, trying to find a life-enriching order

This, perhaps, sounds pompous, but think of a very
common example – Bloomsbury of fifty years ago
against the meander plan of many a town extension.
Then think of some typical non-space between housing blocks, covered with a grass filling because something must be done with it, and then think of the
regulated spaces of Perret's Le Havre (which has to
be experienced) where street widths, building plots,
buildings and open spaces are part of the same order
rather than spaces left over after a road plan has been
established

I recollect Auden's poem beginning 'Sir, no man's
enemy, forgiving all' and ending 'Harrow the house of
the dead; look shining at new styles of architecture,
a change of heart' and know that in the late thirties
and during the war these images sustained many of
us and we saw ourselves as social reformers – apostles
of light in a gloomy world. Fortified by this naïve
role and with some ready-made building forms, we
have produced the characteristic building pattern of
the last years – our mixed developments of slabs and
towers set in what can only be called fall-out space –
a long way from that pre-war image of crystalline
buildings in glorious parkland

We should be chastened when we look at the outcome of our hastily formed images and wise enough
to see that we are still at it. Now we're all in love
with the casbah image which will soon be turned
into the mega-spread, latest in the line, and equally
exploitable. Perhaps it is that we're incapable of
influencing events and these are socio-economic
forms which happen willy-nilly by natural selection.
There's some truth in it maybe, but I think we're too
conceited and build new ideas before we've assimi-
lated them, want too much to hit the headlines with
trend-setting and size. The team follows suit and we
even have colour supplement consultants and surveyors briskly rattling their computers as they talk
about built environment – they also are fallible

Which came first, the Parthenon, or Pallas Athena?
We're told that the Greeks were too sensible to
think in terms of 'either – or', with them it was not
only / but also

Not only planning but also organizing. Not only
function but also form. Not only structure
but also the expression of structure. Not only
shelter but also significance, housing but also
home. And so on, a nice game, which perhaps points
a moral – our failure to see a problem because we
are already in love with our answer. Art, as well
as science, finds out

I fear that this is turning into a conflation of non-
sequiturs. However, I think, put simply, I'm saying
we are concerned in our work with 'head, heart and
hands'

From the head, finding out, understanding, organizing and structuring. From the heart the creative act,
the knowing, the feeling, the giving. From the hands
the putting together, the sensing of material, the
pleasure of making, of a thing well-made. Thus
(rather than become polarized), we try to bring all
our faculties together instead of allowing our co-
ordinating role to take precedence over our form-
giving function – using form in the wide sense of total
ordering, always bounded by materials

The alternative, it seems, is that we are controlled by
events, bounded by economics, we only have to
juggle around the elements needed in a building and
we have it. A sort of inevitability of history attitude
– say, balance of alternatives design. Rather, for me,
architecture implies resolution of human needs and
building requirements (in the context of the wider
environment) through a conception of interior
spaces and external forms, their appropriate structure
and expression, so that the totality has indivisible
formal significance greater than the sum of the parts.
At the same time embodying technical requirements
within a sound fabric realized in authentic materials

All this seems far removed from the business of
running a practice. To client and contractor our
primary role may appear as management, so that at
times it may be necessary to be covert about our
wider functions. However, building is a reciprocal
process and we develop each other's faculties – our
own, our collaborators, our clients private and public.
If the latter, it is more difficult, for in a committee
situation belief has to be imparted and sustained

Thus our dual role – apart from the creative side,
we have to provide what perhaps stems from belief
and the initial conception, the moral energy for a
project, we have to initiate action and keep on
initiating it through thick and thin, until the realization is complete. To me the dual roles seem integral
and divorce between creation and realization
(design – production) undesirable. Head, heart and
hands are part of the same body. Yet this seems to be
a minority view, perhaps because it takes time and
patience. I find stimulus in the process of building,
believing that the realization of a design should be a
joyful end to an act of faith for which we accept the
necessary intermediate stages of work and labour

However, when I was first asked to talk in this series, the year before last, I had barely become a jet-set architect, faced with a large commission (a conference centre and hotel) in Saudi Arabia. In fact, I started notes for this talk waiting at an airport to take off for Riyadh and I realized that I had found myself in a position that I had always distrusted (not air travel) – faced with the problems of a larger office after having worked the last fifteen years or so at a modest scale, with everything more or less under personal control. However, I hope I am wise enough not to be seduced by the quantitative fallacy, however much I am told I am nationally a good thing through the export of know-how. I am aware of a certain expansion price that has to be paid, just as nationally we'll have to pay in other ways for some of our more resounding projects. Fred Pooley's talk[2] was heartening to me for its quizzical look at systems and consortia and concern that building in the traditional sense, which still has infinite resources to offer, is being discarded in our honeymoon with the slick-click, the inevitable post and panel (you choose the infilling material from a wide range of attractive finishes). Ironically, the loved child of both prophets of a new order and profit-makers of the old

I now draw on Maxwell Fry:

'The acceptance of the mediocre as the best life offers is indeed a danger insufficiently recognized. If I were to say that architecture suffers from the same myopic view of its responsibilities you would know that I speak the truth and would see the justice in the public's condemnation of matchbox architecture. Yet we are so much in the grip of the reproductive system as we are the agents of a bureaucracy whether governmental or commercial and the buildings we design must reflect the character of both, which makes the task of creating the background that responds to the deeper levels of human consciousness that much more difficult'[3]

I believe our main contribution is what we build and truly it is not the size of what we do but the quality of thought that matters. For instance, Aldo van Eyck's small playgrounds in Amsterdam transformed what were regarded as waste plots awaiting some jam-tomorrow scheme into living places which helped regenerate parts of a city

The modest Maison Cook had a potency beyond its size, transmuted the domestic into the sublime. There is a time to be noble and a time to be modest, or just innocent – which doesn't mean relaxing

thought but possibly intensifying it to find what can be discarded and what is appropriate in a limited situation

Happily for our national pride, apart from the Crystal Palace, it is customary to show the nineteenth century English domestic school from Philip Webb onwards as our contribution to the developing stream of 'modern'. I'm sure no-one was more surprised than Voysey when he was hailed as a pioneer of that of which he disapproved. Nevertheless, the architectural history industry has cultivated a nice genealogical tree which connects everything of interest but which tends to show an object's place in time as of more importance than its other characteristics. Perhaps this was necessary to give modern architecture respectable parentage but it illustrates the workings of what Wyndham Lewis called the 'demon of progress in the arts'

It was easy to patronize those fine architects for their apparent prophecy, for their unknowing place in space/time – 'good fellows, so modern you know, if only they'd had our technology and forward-looking ideas'. It would be better to know something more about their buildings for I wonder if we should not re-assess those pre-first war architects and pick up the threads of what was a building movement and let drop a little the art/social revolution threads we have held so long. Look at their buildings as fabrics again and question the accepted view as too symmetrical, too much out of the library

In the same vein, and later, our historians see 'de Stijl' as of seminal influence. No doubt it was, but with some diffidence I wonder at the general effect in our time of this painter-dominated movement. The spatial thing was important, but was it not there already? Stylistically (at a superficial level perhaps), but immensely pervasive, the influence seems nothing but baleful. Directing attention again away from buildings as constructed of tangible material exposed to weather and people, to building as plastic art, painting and eventually as graphics. At the end of the line as photographs, light and shade, pattern, not form, surface, not structure and material

This sort of building design is omnipresent. Those who see it as inevitable, the result of the system, advocate more art works to provide frisson to monotony. Consortia add artists to their teams to look after visual effects, colour consultants, textural advisers – so our brave start ends in mosaic and cladding, in a watery dilution of 'neo-plasticism'

So gradually we seem to divest ourselves of ou functions, verbalizing the while about our need seek new comprehensive roles as sociologists, technists, but ending, perhaps, just as beautici

As individuals and professionals we might know we want to do ultimately, but meanwhile we m relax a little, forget our public image and make s prosaic buildings. Good prose is structured, cog lucid without redundancies. Perhaps we should poetry come of its own accord or at least think art doesn't always have to be eloquent to endu

'... He who without betraying the materials nor requirements of today, will have produced a w which seemed to have always existed, a work w in one word, is banal. I say, he will be able to con himself satisfied. The object of art is not to surp or move us ... but to lead us dialectically from s faction to satisfaction and beyond admiration to placid delectation'[4]

Thus Perret, with his continuing preoccupation the constant. Then in painting: 'Is it not precise Piero's ineloquence, his unemotional, unfeeling figures, behaving as if nothing could touch them in short, his avoidance of inflation, which in tim exasperated passions rests, calms and soothes th spectator and compels gratitude and worship'[5]

To read the journals, those narcissistic packages all love, you might think that the design of build or environment is some kind of inter-disciplina struggle where the architect, rather than be lea sets problems for others to solve and then refer the match

'Team' is too often an advertiser's concept. By OED it means two or more beasts of burden ha nessed together. I know in our context it means of persons working together, but I guess it is m often thought of as a metaphor from sport, espec organized sport, of which I am not enamoured. Games, yes, because there is no end product, o play. But who are our opponents I wonder? Intra material, money, clients, or the lot?

No, it won't do. On the other hand we can't w on our own. I do believe we have to understand d extend our observation of techniques rather tha abandon certain areas. We must in a sense know things work and appreciate the contributions of others, realizing their significance in relation to whole as we discern it. Also, we have, sometime

...ake others perform, and sometimes say, 'my ...'s made up, don't confuse me with facts'. We ... to remind everyone, including ourselves that ...g professional doesn't just mean doing our jobs ... extraordinary competence, but means trying ...erve society while carrying out our immediate ...es to our clients. An impossible ideal, but to be ...ed for. You might say that society is often our ...t nowadays. Not so. The State, the local authority ...ide the means, but the society we serve ...sists of people, all of us, in some sort of ...tionship

...orking for some authorities, we are fortunate when ... get well-prepared instructions and there is ...hitectural understanding. Working for private ...nts is also attractive in that there are real people ...o want something, there is the stimulus of dis-...sion, mutual education, even. On the other hand, ...vate clients who want only so many units of ...eculative floor space or generalized accommodation ...ovide little spur to the imagination, even though ...onomy can provide a sort of flaggelant stimulus. ...e outcome of this situation often seems to be a sort ...architectural 'wonderloaf'. This seems an area in ...ich teams operate, often within the industry. Then ...e hired architect becomes only a speaker about ...corative aesthetics, over-ruled by the accountants

...is situation apart, for good building, somewhere ...hind the democratic front (supported doubtless, ... many teams whether consciously or unconsciously ...rmed) there is someone who needs to produce a ...hole building, who is aware of most issues involved ...d who comprehends at many levels, 'a paragon who ...st cannot exist', whatever his professional suffixes, ...e Architect. In control, which includes financial ...ontrol. That I take to mean deciding where material ... best disposed to produce a correct (architecturally ...formed) solution, that is, providing space to create ...onvenience and ambience and choosing materials ...o structure it. Surrender financial control and ...rchitectural control goes too! Even with control, ...e protest too little about standards as we try to do ...he maximum for the minimum. Caring less about ...hat a thing is, only what it costs and perhaps looks ...ke in a cosmetic sort of way

...So where does one start on a task? I still wonder. ...At the conscious level no doubt, the functional/ ...practical – but at the same time maybe with the vision ...of a space or form, perhaps with a magic image of a ...conjunction of materials and light, or even perhaps ...just the way a window is set in a wall might start the ...reaction

As one goes on, early stages become fused. The clarification of the problems, the accommodation/site equation determine the generating line that is followed. The site, for me, often being the crystal in the saturated solution. Sometimes an idea does spring out of the side of a problem, unsought – maybe wrong. Development in one way is explored, and then stopped for this or that severely practical reason, or because of one's inner censor, that scrupulous watch dog we all must cultivate. Modest problems perhaps solve themselves in the head. The more complex, the greater the need to clarify and establish priorities

Today we have extended from the practical field of economy, services, circulation and function to con-sideration of well-being, psychological as well as physical needs. It is obvious that we can no longer refer just to our intuitions but have to support them with a more informed knowledge of the range of human behaviour

This still only amounts to our terms of reference and the task of resolution almost seems impossible but we have to try and we should be learning as we live and do. Thus at this stage it amounts to: 'Not only thought, not only intuitions, but a terrible amount of disciplined labour.' Until one knows the whole inside and outside. At the level of the problem (the function/folk equation) and eventually at the level of a building (the means/milieu equation) so that one can walk through it, in and out, up and down as if realized

We may start with a conception, or with the breaking down and putting together of parts, often a necessary study, part of the design process. Schedule the accommodation, sort into basic units, put together an arrangement serving convenience, economy, securing appropriate advantage to each unit, at the same time considering structure and services. Such a synthetic result is a reassuring stand-by but one which has to be taken to pieces immediately for recreation as an organic entity. For that structuring which, however we may start, is the essential basis of architecture. I don't mean statics, which has to be consonant with it, but that deeper structuring. The organizational pattern, no – not just that, the organizational/spatial pattern, the Swedish word 'formspräk', that which penetrates a building (or environment) in all dimensions, transmutes the utilitarian into significant order to produce 'the architectural totality, the building task realized within a characteristic formal organization'[6], let's say – a style

Alas, many plans get stuck at the accretive stage – pleased to find something that works, believing in functionalism, we build it, mistaking a tool for the product. Instead, while solving space organization problems we should be trying to create ambience beyond the lab concept of environment. Something to which we respond beyond comfort and well-being, a milieu which connects us to the poetry of living, heightening our awareness of today as part of yester-day and the day before yesterday, rather than, say, romantically orientating to some quite unknown future. This is what I understand to be organic architecture

In planning, one gradually acquires a certain modesty regarding use. At a personal level, how often do one's own home arrangements fail in use. How long does it take to admit the garden is an adventure play-ground, or that something we use is wrongly designed or chosen. Thus Ken Bayes's 'Therapeutic effect of environment on disturbed children'[7] makes a point beyond his chosen limits. We're all disturbed, in a sense, and we need to understand response to space, form and material at a profounder level – while admitting that misuse is probably a mistake on our part

We have to satisfy the physical requirements ('you are an organizer, not a drawing board stylist') often in an open-ended way. Just at one moment, perhaps, our plans correspond to needs, but who knows the future?

So we do perhaps begin to consider more the milieu-creating role of architecture, the whole environment inside and out. What about the symbolizing role? That which Loos saw so clearly when he wrote: 'When we discover a mound in the woods six feet long and three feet wide and shaped in the form of a pyramid we become serious and something inside us says "here someone lies buried, this is archi-tecture" '

'Architecture becomes symbolic or monumental in giving visual expression to the constitutive ideas of a community or to the social structure'[6]

We cannot ignore it since we are more clearly informed about its importance in the past, for instance, the patronizing image of gothic architecture as a sort of early structural functionalism has been destroyed or we no longer need see the Parthenon's peripteral structure as the vestige of some yet undiscovered prototype but even may see it as a symbol of the sacred grove in which the cella building once stood

Yet to cultivate the symbolic might be worse than ignoring it, for already in the absence of an accepted hierarchy of values we inflate the currency (for example, too many student residences have been college symbols rather than domestic buildings). On the other hand, there are moments when we have to raise the local into the national thus I think fellow architects are wrong to attack Sydney, which was such a situation. The tragedy there, perhaps, was having the right architecture for the wrong building object. Much as I care for opera, the opera house as symbol is a nineteenth-century concept, but what a fabulous plan!

Schultz speaks of the functional-practical, milieu creating and the symbolizing function of architecture. Aside, it interests me to think of a basic statement such as a bridge. There is the functional-practical artefact, military or railway, any old bridge. Bridge as an incident. We can have a milieu-creating bridge, Ponte Vecchio or old London Bridge. And there are bridges as symbols. For instance, Tower Bridge – most powerful of examples, how well it works both ways – up the Thames under it, gateway to the port or the sea; across it, splendid entrance to the City. An architectural/engineering totality, possibly more important now than that chilly old greenhouse that burned down in Sydenham

Finally, and needless to say, the process of design includes the injection into the development of our technical 'know-how' of ways and means, making a sound roof and a dry basement. We must accept building as our bedrock, know it inside and out, be dissatisfied with the meanness of our minimum standards, we have to look again at what is called traditional for 'We are continually harping on what is different in our time to such an extent that we lose touch with what is not different, what is essentially the same'

Thus, through countless overlapping stages, imperceptibly we should bring architectural/technical order to the whole and to the parts:

'And every phrase and sentence that is right
(Where every word is at home,
Taking its place to support the others,
The word neither diffident nor ostentatious,
An easy commerce of the old and new,
The common word exact without vulgarity,
The formal word precise but not pedantic,
The complete consort dancing together)'[8]

I have tried to stress what I regard as the duality of our activity, maybe I'm too practical for the poetic or too poetic for the practical. Nevertheless, let me end unabashed with this from Stuart Hampshire: 'Maturity as an aim of education demands an integral intelligence which is at ease both with factual investigations of reality and also with wild but ordered and significant reconstructions of it'[9]

Postscript

It seems appropriate to print this piece which, re-read after three years, appears to be a 'plea for quality' and still relevant to the building scene

Now I feel more inclined to stress how, apart from conscious sources, one draws on those unconscious sources that are part of one's personal equipment, nurtured over years ever since one began being an architect, through work, travel, buildings old and new, the arts and life itself. All that nurtures the creative imagination, enabling one to see things afresh and perhaps more whole. It is this unseen, almost unacknowledged because (in today's climate of opinion) unquantifiable quality, that ultimately constitutes our authority as architects and which seems to be forgotten in our pursuit of new passions such as sociology and technology

[1] 18 Lectures on Industrial Society, Raymond Aron, Weidenfeld and Nicholson
[2] RIBA Journal, March 1968
[3] Housing and the Environment, E. Maxwell Fry, RIBA Journal, August 1967
[4] Perret, quoted by E. Goldfinger, Architects' Year Book 7, 1956
[5] Piero della Francesca, B. Berenson, Chapman and Hall
[6] Intentions in Architecture, N. Schultz, Allen and Unwin
[7] Kaufmann International Design Award Study, Kenneth Bayes, published by the author
[8] Little Gidding, Eliot
[9] A Ruinous Conflict, Stuart Hampshire, New Statesman, 4 May 1962

...ard Church house completion, Kent 1950

...house was originally an oast house group
...sting of two square and two circular kilns
...ther with a connecting barn

...lly, one of the square kilns was demolished
...the other converted into a double height
...g room and over this the owner's study.
...ground floor of the barn was converted into
...g room, kitchen, bedroom and bathroom
...two bedrooms in the circular kilns at first
...level

...completion was entirely concerned with the
...n and consisted of planning two new bedrooms
...bathrooms in the upper part, spiral stair to
...study from the principal bedroom and altering
...ground floor to provide main entrance, hall,
...ended kitchen and improved stairs

...oughout the design the simple character and
...ce of the old building has been retained – by
...ect rather open planning with glazed screens
...doors, by exposing as much of the main
...ucture as possible and avoiding in material and
...ail a conventional 'upholstered' approach.
...e luxury is in spaciousness and clarity – qualities
...eady beautifully established in the original
...nversion completed in 1939 by the Berlin
...chitect, F. L. Marcus

...oking centre, London 1954

...rt of the second floor of an existing building was
...nverted into a centre for the testing and
...monstration of the use of a vegetable fat. The
...commodation consists of:

...demonstration room planned to take advantage
...the existing curved window wall which, forming
...e rear wall, faces the demonstration platform
...ith cookers, working space, etc.

...kitchen (and demonstration area) separated by
...lazed screens and doors from a central reception
...rea. An office for the director, placed between the
...rincipal rooms has a solid door and panel, which
...arry an enlarged reversed photograph of a pack
...s it appears before folding into carton

...A suspended ceiling covers the whole area, but
...excluding the demonstration area (where the
...existing beams assisted the form of the room) and
...excluding throughout a narrow strip adjoining

Section: bedroom, study, living room

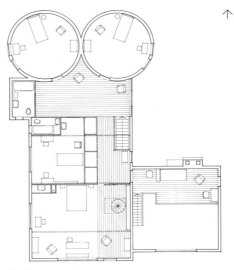

Bedroom level

Landing, view towards circular bedrooms

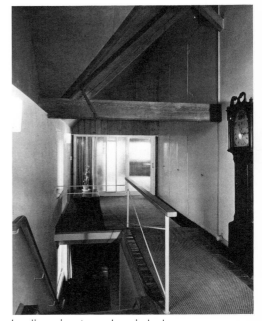

Landing, view towards main bedroom

Church house, main bedroom, looking towards entrance and stair to study

outside wall. Lighting is incorporated into
strip

e kitchen is divided into two areas by the
r – height projecting storage unit which
eens washing – up from the entrance area which
ends to form a spectator's space distinct
m the working area and fitted with a display
ent

atially, great care was taken to achieve unity
d connection through the whole area, by use of
zed screens, by the lowered ceiling, by the
e of a continuing colour for the outside wall in
h room, by the arrangement of the light
tings to connect the principal rooms with the
trance area, while different floor materials
ticulate the main areas

ea bar, Festival of Britain 1951

tuated at first floor level in the middle of
dustrial displays, the design maintained the open
eling of the pavilion while establishing a different
haracter appropriate to a refreshment area

stair and a balcony edge bounded the space on
vo long sides which was then articulated by
uspended overlapping ceiling planes related to
he different areas of use

he entrance area, defined by the lowest canopy,
vas adjacent to the compact self-service unit.
he main space divided into standing table area
owards the balcony side and, nearer the stair side,
he sitting area – this covered by the main
anopy, the two 'solid' ceilings being linked by a
emi-transparent intermediate ceiling over the
main service counter area. Further space definition
was provided by table shelves, screens and flower
boxes and lighting features

Chapel, Maze Hill, London 1954

This small chapel was formed within existing
church buildings as a 'sanctuary' until a new church
could be built to replace one destroyed by the
war. The project and the chapel have since been
abandoned

Being at the rear of the site and at a lower level
than the street, a high raised canopy was used to
mark the entrance. The approach was not direct and
the visitor crossing the first terrace was 'turned'
by a brick sculpture and a bench, then went

Cooking centre, kitchen looking towards entrance

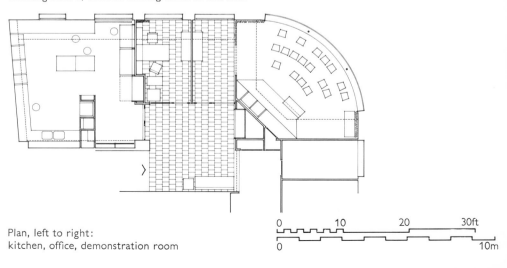

Plan, left to right:
kitchen, office, demonstration room

0   10   20   30ft

0   10m

by a sloping path and steps down to a brick paved terrace forming a small concourse at the entrance

The chapel had an aisle on one side only with a lowered slab over, supported by rods from the ceiling and spanning the room. These and the slab, which reflected light on to the main ceiling, increased the apparent height of the room and the rods helped to 'regulate' the space

The plan shows both proposed new church and the chapel as built

Reception area, London 1958

Reception, waiting and general secretarial space was required within an existing room for Lund Humphries' London office. The room was restored as far as possible to its original Georgian character and new work inserted as free elements. These consisted of:

a shaped reception counter with a pass gate; a timber screen (supported by a circular column with attached lighting) forming a sitting area with two fixed seats and a low table; a floating lowered ceiling over the public area. The ceiling consisted of slats at two levels and different spacings spanning between two deep side members. A mural panel was envisaged as the only area for applied colour and as a feature in relation to the waiting space, rising through the 'open' ceiling. Patrick Heron's work at that time was in accord with the idea – bands of colour in the painting and the slats of the ceiling at two levels bring the two elements into close relationship. (The specially commissioned painting is now in the Tate Gallery)

Reception area, Bradford 1955

Part of the ground floor of Lund Humphries' existing administration building (stone walls, timber floors and beams, cast iron columns) re-planned as an entrance, waiting and exhibition space, etc.

The entrance area is divided with door height glazed screens into lobby with adjacent porter's and receptionist's rooms. The main area comprises a waiting space which extends into an exhibition space and interview bays which correspond to the structural grid and are formed by L-shaped screens. Apart from natural side light, ceiling lighting consists of alternate lines of tungsten and fluorescent light, screened by simple hanging louvres

Entrance, looking towards sitting area, service on left

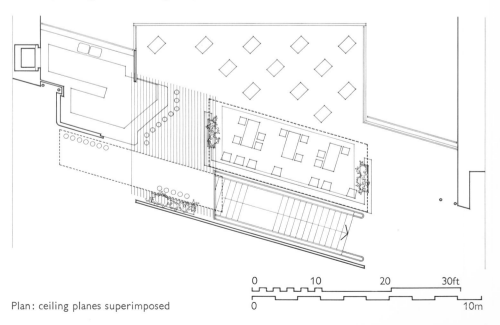

Plan: ceiling planes superimposed

| 0 | 10 | 20 | 30ft |
| 0 | | | 10m |

Chapel, interior looking towards pulpit

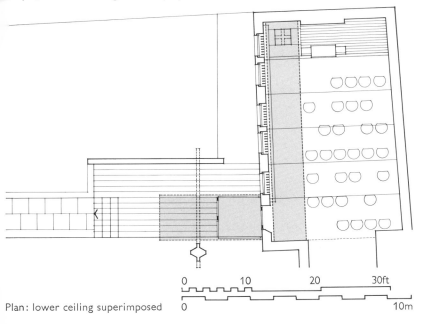

Plan: lower ceiling superimposed

0 10 20 30ft

0 10m

Reception area London, sitting recess and screen

Entrance and mural panel

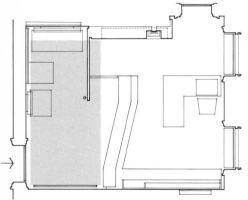

Plan: louvred ceiling superimposed

Reception area Bradford: general view, interview bays, showcase and mural panel

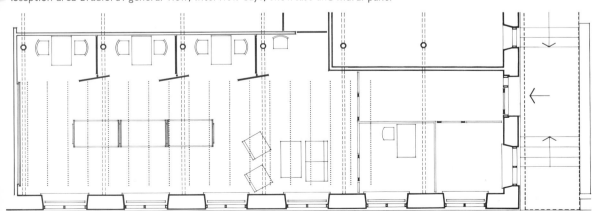

Plan: hanging louvres superimposed

between each row, which give the effect of a lowered ceiling. The louvres are divided into three sections painted different colours to a particular overall rhythm. The colours are related to the richer colours in the collage (constructed from waste printed material) by E. Paolozzi which forms a feature on the end wall of the room, terminating the perspective of the ceiling

Installation, Jackson Pollock exhibition, London 1958

A special layout and presentation was prepared to accommodate the travelling exhibition of Jackson Pollock's paintings organized by the Museum of Modern Art

An interlocking sub-division of the main space of the Whitechapel Gallery was generated by the placing of four screen walls of rough block painted white and forming an appropriate background for some of the paintings. Black and grey fabric was stretched over part of the existing wall areas and screens of untreated wood were introduced for special emphasis. A white fabric ceiling over the main area of the gallery helped to unify and emphasize the central space of the gallery, with the cross dimension emphasized by floor matting

Architecture exhibition 1956

This installation for the Arts Council was within an 18th-century interior and attempted to create, by use of screens and velariums, space equivalents to the experience of modern architecture. Special display screens were also designed at the same time for this and other exhibitions

Pollock exhibition, view across central space towards entrance

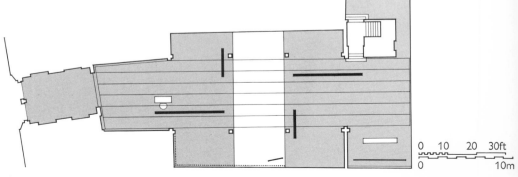

Plan: showing spatial sub-division

entral space and four screen walls

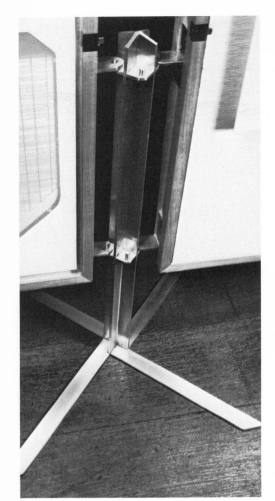

Architecture exhibition, detail of screen

General view of main exhibition room

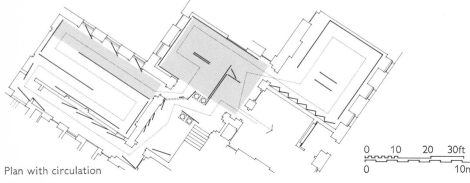

Plan with circulation

0 10 20 30ft

0 10m

...gregational Church, Blackheath 1957

...er than build a temporary church after
...olition of the 19th-century war-damaged shell,
...tually new church was created out of part of
...old fabric, retaining sections of three walls and
...structing a new roof over the reduced volume
... axis at right angles to the old one. What
... the end wall, with fine organ (retained) became
... solid side wall of the new building, the
...osite wall consisting entirely of glazing between
... massive stone piers

... church is approached through a courtyard
...in that area of the old building not incorporated
... the church, formed by retaining parts of the
... walls as enclosing screens. The courtyard is
...tly gravelled as a 'concourse' and separated from
... church by a raised garden. From the 'concourse'
...ps lead to the entrance porch which breaks
...ough the lower part of the first bay. On the
...rtyard side, the structure is entirely new, only
... ends show how the new building and courtyard
...into the old shell. The two piers support trusses
...rying the low pitched slated roof. The ridge is
...t central but towards the organ side and the
...of carries down lower on the courtyard side with
...eep eaves and fascia

...ating is planned as a central block with aisles
...her side. The pulpit is central to the ridge line
...d set on a brick platform which also carries the
...mmunion table and the font. The interior, as in
...raditional parish church, depends on simple
...ms and ordinary materials. The main walls are
...t the white of lime plaster, the stone piers are
...surfaced and the timber trusses and roof
...nstruction are undecorated, providing with the
...ne wood block floor a warm contrast to the walls.
...he side glazing is clear, the courtyard can be
...en from within and in a sense the two spaces are
...ited making one more aware of the relationship
...f the old to the new

General view from courtyard, glazed wall between piers

Section: church and courtyard

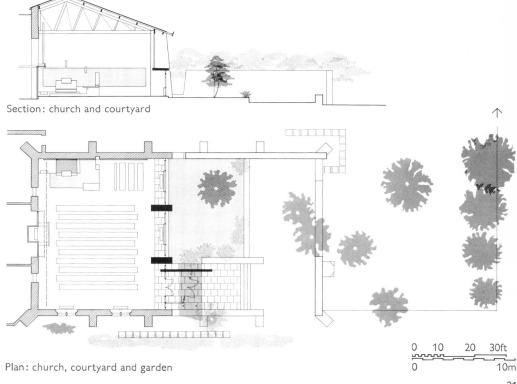

Plan: church, courtyard and garden

0 10 20 30ft

0   10m

General view of church from courtyard at night

...one piers, lower and upper glazing, looking towards entrance

View from entrance toward organ and pulpit

Dobbs house, London NW3, 1958

The site was formerly part of a large garden which had been chopped up into a few plots by the vendors

A new access road ends in a turning circle some twelve feet lower than the adjacent side of the site which otherwise falls to the south-east. The awkward shape of the site and the need to screen future building to the south led to the T-shaped plan with the living room principally orientated east and west, embracing the garden on one side and opening out on to the terrace over the garage on the other

The approach to the house is by steps broken into easy stages with changes of direction. The terrace is at a higher level than the path and screened by planting. Past the north flank wall a turn through 180° leads to the front door, recessed in a porch

The house is divided by the hall and stairway giving access to all the rooms as well as to the garden. The formal arrangement and the structure follow this division on both floors – the entrance porch and living-room porch correspond with narrow terraces at first floor level. The west block contains living room and study with three bedrooms over, the east block includes dining room and kitchen, etc., with principal bedroom and bathrooms over

On the south side, the splayed flank wall follows the line of the south boundary and visually the living room area extends on the east side into the porch under the first floor balcony and the garden beyond. The main space is sub-divided to form living room and study by the projecting fireplace wall

West side of house, garage and entrance steps

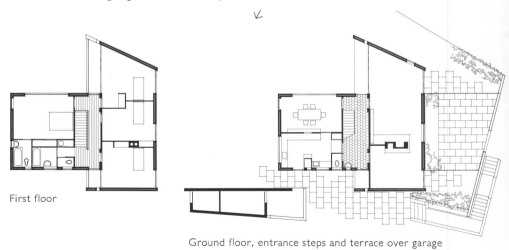

First floor

Ground floor, entrance steps and terrace over garage

```
0    10    20   30ft
0              10m
```

...ett house, Cambridge 1958

...clients' preference for an upper level living
...m and a dip in the site, led to the sectional
...ngement of garage and boiler room slightly
...w ground floor level with the living room over,
...he half landing of the stairs. On the ground
...r are entrance lobby, toilet, playroom, kitchen
...in the centre, the dining room out of which
...stairs lead, extending the space visually to the
...g room at half-landing level, through the
...ed screen that separates it from the staircase

...horter flight of stairs leads to the central
...ridor and the four bedrooms and bathroom,
...pactly planned around it. The ceiling level
...nds over the living room, which thus has extra
...ght

...e form of the upper part of the house corre-
...nds to the structural change which provides
...itional space at bedroom and living room levels,
...also, considering the fall of the site away from
...e road and the view from there, provides the
...cessary architectural emphasis. The lower part,
...ich is constructed of blockwork, is painted a
...ar-black green, while the dominant, slightly
...er-hanging upper part is faced with western red
...dar boarding, weathered to silver-grey

...ort bore piles and ground beams carry the
...ecial insulating structural block walls, which stop
...first floor level. In the living room, the top of
...e wall extends round three sides as a continuous
...l, covered with black tiles. The upper external
...alls are timber framed and lined with plaster-
...ard in the bedrooms and with horizontal
...estern hemlock boarding in the living room and
...aircase

South-west corner of house, main window of living room

Section

0   10   20   30ft

0   10m

Bedrooms and living room floor

Ground floor

Entrance side of house, corner window of living room

Dining room with glazing open

Dining room and bedroom floor, from living room

View to dining room from stair, bedroom floor over, living room right

Plante house, London NW3, 1960

The long, narrow site rises about ten feet from front to back. The clients' expressed preference for living at one level, which with the impossibility of maintaining the scale of the large houses on either side and the need to give good orientation to various rooms while enjoying the garden, led to a one-storey, semi-courtyard plan

The house 'looks in' but it exploits every 'outlook' with cross views from one part to another, giving a special interest and character. Scarcely noticeable from the street the house appears as a low block set between existing houses, different in scale, screened by enclosing walls and trees

The approach to the house is by a screened drive-in on the north-east side, and the centre of the house breaks forward to form the main entrance on one side and the kitchen entrance on the other, while a glazed roof forms a car port

The house consists of a bedroom wing, a living-room wing and a connecting central space which contains a garden room and the kitchen

The entrance lobby leads into the garden room where on one side a step leads up to the bedroom wing, on the other, four steps lead up to the main level (and beyond, the living room). The garden room links the two wings but also serves as an informal dining or sitting area, entirely glazed and with direct access to the sheltered courtyard

From the garden room a large opening leads into the living-room wing. This is one space, with a high ceiling at the entrance, sloping towards the rear of the house. The space is sub-divided by low solid walls, with glazing over to form an L-shaped room for formal dining and sitting and a separate small study. There are windows on three sides giving excellent sunlight penetration and an intriguing variety of views. With the exception of the plastered partition between the two rooms, all the walls are fairfaced brickwork painted white. The sloping ceiling is lined with pine boarding, left natural. The floor is teak block

The bedroom wing is at the front of the site and all bedrooms face east onto a courtyard. There are four small bedrooms, two of which can be thrown together, and one large bedroom, set back from the general line, so forming a sheltered paved area in front of the main window

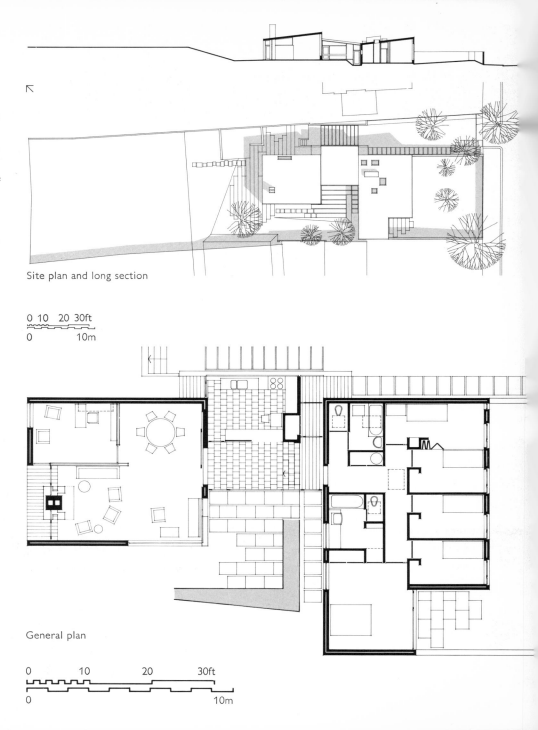

Site plan and long section

0 10 20 30ft

0 10m

General plan

0 10 20 30ft

0 10m

28

Entrance drive, front door and car port

Living-room wing from garden

The garden room from courtyard

29

College and museum, Leicester 1962

Vaughan College provides non-vocational adult
education with many courses in diverse subjects.
Originally a working men's college, founded in
1862 by the Reverend Vaughan, it has played a
considerable part in the life of the city* – it does so
now as a centre of the Department of Adult Education of the University

It is built on the site of what has been regarded as
the 'forum' of Roman Leicester – to the north and
west of the preserved foundations of a surmised
Roman bath, forming a virtual courtyard that en-
hances the setting of the Roman remains (which
include the adjacent and impressive Jewry Wall) and
that visually extends to embrace the close by
church and churchyard

In using the site for the college, it was stipulated
that a museum should be included in the design,
which is consequently based on two levels. The
museum at 'forum' level (ten feet below street) and
at upper level (five feet above street) the main wing
of the college intermediate to the two floors of
the classroom wing to the north

To the south the main floor of the college extends
as a terrace, reached by steps from the street, open
to the public and giving a prospect of the whole site
as well as being the approach to the main entrance.
A stair from the street leads down to a terrace at
'forum' level and the entrance to the museum, which
occupies all the space under the main wing of the
college

The more diverse elements of the college accommodation are planned in the main wing and these
are linked by a flowing common space which varies
in width according to different requirements.
Thus, at the entrance it forms a foyer to the
assembly hall, then a concourse (with adjacent balcony) opposite the office; finally, it expands considerably and, defined by a U-shaped enclosing wall,
forms a common room, the main social room
regarded as a major element, second only in importance to the eight classrooms, which are on two
floors approached by stairs beyond the common
room, half a flight up or down, and then entered off
corridors (with cloaks recesses) on the north side

*'Vaughan College Leicester 1862–1962'
A.J. Allaway, Leicester University Press

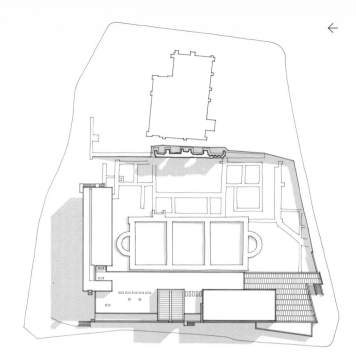

Site plan showing college, forum, Jewry Wall and St Nicholas

Section

College floor plan

0 10 30 60 90ft

0 10 30m

Museum with social wing of college over, seen from beneath classroom wing looking towards entrances

Raised terrace approach to college, assembly hall

The closed space of the library is planned for con
from the general office. Primarily top-lit, it rise
through a double height and a light steel gallery
provides access to the upper shelves

The assembly hall seats 230 and can be used in-
dependently, its foyer being part of the main
entrance area. A small stage has dressing room a
other provisions at the rear. The roof is spanned
with laminated timber beams at close centres

The City of Leicester Museums is responsible for
the Jewry Wall museum, consisting basically of th
space between 'forum' level and the underside of t
main wing of the college and devoted to ancient
and Roman history. It opens on to the 'forum'
with its grassed spaces between the old walls an
looks towards Jewry Wall and St Nicholas Churc
as this side of the space consists of continuous
glazing, breaking forward and back to avoid a
straight demarcation between museum and site, a
opening on to a covered terrace space

A total floor area of some 8,500 sq.ft has been pro
vided in one undivided space, which, architecturall
is dominated by a system of white-painted reinforc
ed concrete barrel vaults which are carried on
transverse double concrete beams at 40ft centres
(the same bay as that of the Roman buildings). Th
structure forms a 'table' from which the college
part with its very varied spaces is built of load-
bearing brick or block wall construction, supporting lightweight steel beams carrying roofing slabs

View of museum from stair down to entrance. Forum with classroom wing beyond

The museum area, glazing to forum on left

Stair down from street to museum

The college library

Library, council chamber, University of Leicester 1964-65

These major interior schemes are within the old central building of the University, where large areas became available upon removal of departments into new buildings

Council chamber

The council suite is in the heart of the building and includes the ante-room, an adjacent committee room and the chamber proper. This was formerly a chapel and a pitched suspended timber ceiling has been inserted to provide a scale more appropriate to the new use. Natural light is introduced through windows on one side at high level and the ceiling is 'dormered' to accommodate this. It was thought essential to have a symmetrical room and an equivalent row of windows has been introduced on the opposite side. These, however, are false and provided with simulated daylight. The geometry of the ceiling is realized in western hemlock boarding left natural and waxed. Existing wall panelling in oak is retained, the floor is carpeted in seaweed green. New tables were designed to go with existing high-back chairs

The library

Stage 1 of an extension scheme provides a capacity of 200,000 volumes and 450 reading places

The building was constructed in the early nineteenth century as an asylum and was only partially converted for university use after 1920. Much of the structural work in the library consisted of the removal of cross walls – destroying the old 'cell' planning – to give larger bays for book space and for reading, and for common spaces such as the entrance hall

The library entrance was moved to the centre of the side of the building nearest the major development area of the site, leading into a central entrance (with central stairs) from which wings extend in three directions on two floors

In general, planning is based on open access with sections of closely spaced stack adjacent to sections of wider spaced bookcases arranged to form reading bays

The entrance hall was formed by freeing existing spaces and stripping back to basic structure, within

Council chamber, existing panelling restored, new ceiling and 'dormer' lighting

il of timber ceiling, 'dormers' and lighting

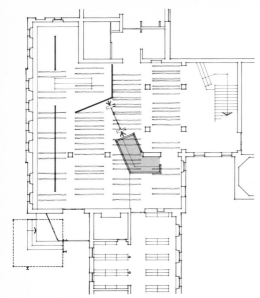

Library, plan of entrance area

```
0    10    20    30ft
|--|--|--|--|--|--|
0              10m
```

which various free-standing elements have been
placed to screen cloaks area and form directional
walls, to form a porter's kiosk and barriers to
provide controlled entrance and exit

The ceiling consists of 'boxes' containing fluorescent
or tungsten fittings, or plain. Spanning between
steel sections below the old ceiling, the boxes can
be adjusted in position to give a close or open
effect and this arrangement has been used to
emphasize the route to the inner entrance hall

The stair is visually separated from the first floor
central space (issue and return counter, catalogues,
etc.) by a showcase for the display of books, manu-
scripts, etc. Returning back over the stair is the entrance to the central reading room of the old library

In general, the design is based on 'stripping back'
to basic spaces and structure and sub-dividing by
screens, bookcases, etc. The original spaces as
modified provide a diversity and richness that is
rarely attained in a new library. In detail, the utmost
simplicity has been pursued, using lasting materials
with generous and uncomplicated detail

Library, detail of secondary stair

ntrance, control desk and screens to cloaks area

Detail of double sided showcase separating issue area from main stairs

Detail of issue counter

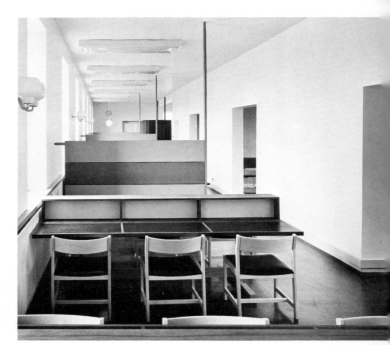

One of the reading rooms

replanning of two separate first floor rooms in
nome of Mr and Mrs J. H. Pedersen included the
rior design and selection of furniture and
ishings

bedrooms have separate entrances from the
way, but are connected by a wide doorway with
oted panel, plus a narrow fixed strip of glass
uring visual continuity. The general carpeting
eaweed green) and the long curtaining (alternate
pes, pale blue and tobacco) are used in both
ms but short curtains are pale blue over the
ssing table in the big room and tobacco over the
k in the smaller room

e door to the small room is recessed in the wall
upboards, the doors of which are finished in
te beech. A fascia panel painted dusky red over
various doors helps to unify the wall. The bed
Il is covered with straw coloured matting, divided
a wood rail which carries bedside light, etc.

e separating wall forms a large cupboard to the
in room. Again, doors are white beech and the
ifying fascia here is purplish blue. Opposite, the
essing table fitment extends the full width of the
om. The centre has a flap-up top with mirror,
vealing a two-depth compartment. The bed wall
covered with 'silver' Japanese grass paper. The
d is a standard steel frame on 'French castors' with
ecially designed panels in dark and light blue
oric

| 0 | | 10ft |
| 0 | | 3m |

Plan

Small room with pivoted door opening into large room

Large bedroom, detail of dressing table

elopment of the University's existing hall of
dence at Cottingham, in which new building
is the major part, providing 80 study bed-
ms, dining hall, kitchen staff and service
ommodation, etc., in a two-storey building
ned to one side of the old building with one
cipal pedestrian entrance at a key point be-
en the two. By appropriate form and scale,
tisfactory relationship between the old and new
gs has been established – giving the sense of one
. Also the village street scale has been respected

building is developed about two courtyards
n towards the old buildings and garden. The
ger court gives access to the residential wings,
considered as the hub of the whole group, from
ich there is access to all the main social rooms
at is, dining hall, senior common room, meeting
m, music room in the new wing, junior common
m, library in the old wing, as well as the
rden's accommodation and the existing residen-
accommodation. The residential courtyard of
new wing is apparent from the entrance court-
d, beyond the projecting part of the dining hall.
e SCR is planned at first floor on the north-west
rner of the social group and opens on one side to
errace which runs along the west side of the
ilding forming a colonnade at ground level

udent accommodation is planned in groups of
om five to eight rooms, each with its own pantry
ut sharing sanitary accommodation planned generally
the ground floor. Thus, sanitary accommodation is
aced with the least favoured aspects on one side of
e ground floor, with study bedrooms on the oppo-
te side, while on the first floor over, study bedrooms
e planned on both sides of a central corridor.
ive north-facing rooms have narrow windows for
utlook and high-level south windows for sunlight

he sanitary accommodation is lit by strip windows
etween the first floor soffit and the lower ex-
ernal walls, which are slightly forward of the
eneral building line. These were conceived as walls
or creepers and climbers – part of the landscape
esign of the courtyard and the street side

The entrance hall is separated by a low barrier
from the dining hall and a stair leads from it to a
gallery off which open a music room, a meeting
room and the senior common room, with windows
on north and west overlooking court and garden

Site model, new building left, old building centre and right

Street side of new building. Kitchen in centre, residential wing beyond

Entrance court, looking past dining hall to residential court. Common room windows over entrance to hall

dential court looking towards dining hall. The main terracing extends as a peninsula into the lower court

The dining hall. Stair to social rooms on left

Detail of stair to social rooms. Common room on right over main entrance

Residential group, Cambridge 1967

A design submitted in limited competition for the development of Trinity College's 'Burrell's Field', an area of old gardens to the north of the University Library

Two main groups of accommodation for under-graduates or fellows are disposed either side of the stream which bisects the site. On the south side, a three-storey building group is arranged to form a square courtyard related to a smaller entrance court off adjacent footways. The accommodation consists of two upper floors of 'sets' of varied size and character – each group related to service and other accommodation at half levels. There are also rooms at courtyard level but in part the building is open and a colonnade on the north side opens on to a long rectangular 'suggested' courtyard formed by a wing of the building and a second L-shaped building which defines the space

A small facilities hall related to the stream and a decorative pool forms a pivotal feature

On the north side of the stream is the second resi-dential group – five 4 to 5 storey units which cluster together and with floors that can be arranged as sets of rooms or as self-contained flats. These are grouped around a central stair in each unit on a rising 'spiral' with access off a number of intermediate landings

The different types of accommodation are reflected in the contrast between the informally clustered group of buildings and the more formal group round the two major courtyards. It was intended to develop the design with a domestic character rather than in the monumental vein which has often been adopted in recent college building

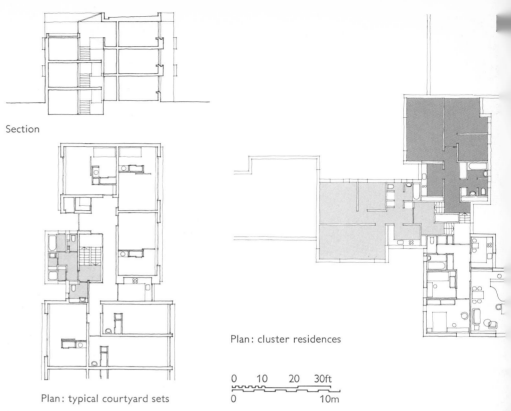

Section

Plan: typical courtyard sets

Plan: cluster residences

```
0    10    20    30ft
0              10m
```

View of model looking across main courtyards to cluster residences

Plan view of model. Entrance bottom right, main courtyard, secondary courtyard with pivotal hall, cluster residences beyond

Trinity Hall Cambridge, Fellows' social building 1964

This new building provides a 'combination room' with 'parlour' over for the Fellows of the college, replacing a previous inadequate one-storey structure and using its site to greater advantage. The combination room is used for meals, for committee meetings, social occasions, recitals, etc. The 'parlour' is used as a retiring-coffee-reading room

The site is very enclosed and natural lighting from the narrow courtyard left by the construction was of particular concern. Despite restrictions, generous well-lit rooms with subtle spatial effects and rich character have been provided and opportunity was taken to realize a complete exterior/interior conception, including furnishings

The combination room is divided into four bays. Three relate to the dining area (and 'parlour' over) the fourth relates to a sitting space centred on a fireplace (and terrace over)

The main space defined on the court side by the columns extends beyond them into a continuous 'bay window' which is divided horizontally by an intermediate slab which, apart from its spatial purpose and effect on scale, helps screen the room from overlooking windows. Its top surface also reflects light into the room

Internal space extends through the lower glazing to the line of a low wall which defines a narrow courtyard which widens opposite the sitting bay

The structure is a concrete frame combined with existing walls. The three columns on the window side support cross-beams between which span oregon pine joists, carrying the boarded double floor of the 'parlour' over. The composite structure is exposed to view as the ceiling over the main part of the combination room. Between the joists lamps are fixed on a random spacing and screened by simple wooden louvre nests. The combination of exposed concrete and timber structure integrated with lighting is richly decorative, giving a warm and convivial quality at night. Lighting over the sitting bay is within a grid of small squares which emphasizes the different space and provides absorption

On the long side of the room, an easy stair (screened by a 'fence-like' balustrade) rises to terrace and 'parlour' which, in contrast, is much more enclosed with a low ceiling and separated from the stair by a screen

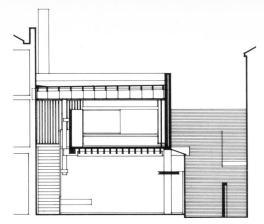

Section

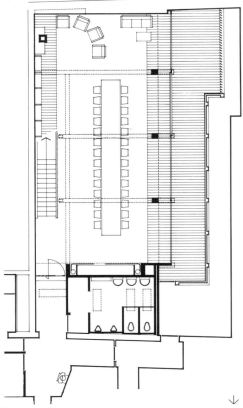

Plan: combination room

Detail of glazing and structure

Courtyard and terrace

bination room, looking towards sitting area. Stair to terrace and parlour

Combination room, sitting area with fireplace

Parlour looking toward terrace, screen to stair

Parlour seen from terrace

Science building and gymnasium, Rosa Bassett School, ILEA London SW17, 1965

The science building is sited east of the existing school and care has been taken to relate to it in scale and character. The two buildings define a courtyard open to the south and the field at lower level. The route from the old building to the new is diagonally across this space, leading naturally into the entrance recessed between the south wing and the centre section

The new building, by its projection, ends the terrace along the south front of the old building and the embankment below it. In a future development this terrace could become a generating route, extending westwards into further buildings and linking old with new. From this follows the siting of the gymnasium, which is so placed that it enjoys a convenient position in relation to the old school and the games pitch – without inhibiting future extension

The gymnasium building consists of two elements – a low block (containing changing rooms, showers, locker room, etc.) principally top lit, and the gym hall. This is the standard size of 70ft × 40ft × 18ft with welded steel frames at 15ft centres, steel purlins, exposed woodwool roof. Clear, uninterrupted end walls are in red brick with concealed strips of top lighting. One side wall is in red brick up to 10ft and above there is glazing on both sides with short returns on the end walls, breaking the rectangular box. The lower wall on the changing room side is faced with white painted boarding. The fixed glazing is clear wired glass, the opening lights in obscured. The floor is yellow beech and all steelwork is painted aluminium. Common materials, rich in conjunction, enhance a taut, fresh space

The science building accommodation is organized on two floors about the rectangular stair hall and its extension. The main rooms consist of general and advanced laboratories for physics, chemistry and biology, plus a lecture room (with stepped floor), together with necessary ancillary accommodation

The architectural-structural organization of this brick and concrete building is in four cells, planned broadly on a 12ft grid: the stair hall and ancillary accommodation; the north end (three bays at right angles to the general line); the centre section (five bays) and, separated by the entrance; the south end (four bays at right angles). Windows stretch from pier to pier and where unpierced walls are

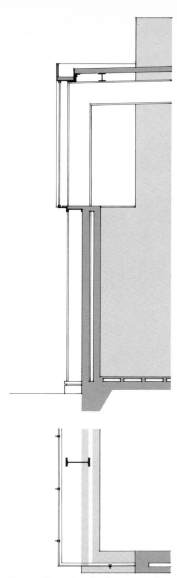

Section

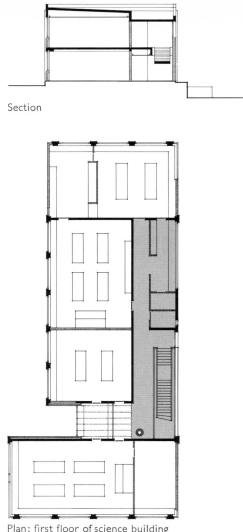

Plan: first floor of science building

Gymnasium, detail of corner, plan and section

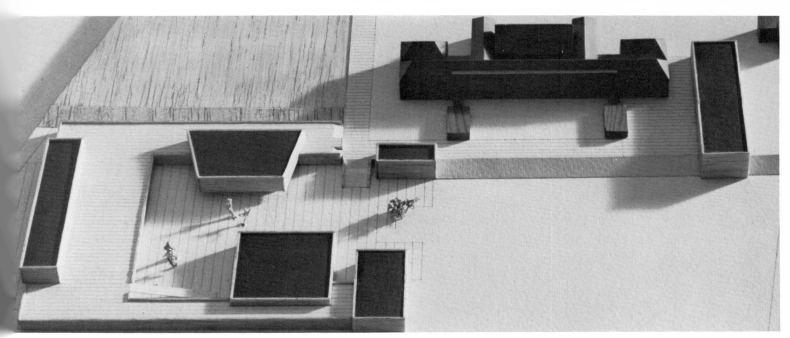

e development model. Gymnasium bottom centre, science building right

Side of gymnasium seen from field

Gymnasium. End wall and glazed corner, outside detail

Inside detail

ired, brick is used as an infill, as also below
ows. The piers rise through the two storeys
carry up to grip the deep concrete roof fascia.
top of this aligns with the adjacent cornice and
piers give a suggestion of the old building

system has been made clear by the apparent
ing in of the piers on the north and south ends,
glazed corners emphasizing the different direc-
of span at the ends of the building. On the
return bays at each end and on the east side
tre) whenever there are extended windows,
planning and structural grid is shown by a
ost' pier (a fixed light window of pier width)

structural system of brick piers controls the
ign on three sides, on the east side the expressed
f pitches and lower height of the stair hall, etc.,
ke clear the general arrangement – the few
t out' window openings in the centre section
mpare with the infill windows to the bay system
the main rooms

building is homogenous – throughout the scale
broad and generous – richness is given by con-
ered profiling and modelling as well as by good
sic materials simply used in depth – as opposed
the meanness of commercial systems with their
ide choice of facing materials at the designer's
scretion'

Gymnasium interior

Science building seen from field

Courtyard formed by science building and old building looking towards science entrance, marked by projecting wing. Field beyond

l of gymnasium. Terrace to old school above embankment on left and science building in distance

Bootham School York, assembly hall, 1971

Bootham is a Society of Friends school for boys. The clients laid down detailed requirements but also indicated the critical architectural problem – that of designing a building of form and atmosphere appropriate to daily assembly and Friends weekly meeting, yet capable of being transformed into one suitable for theatre and opera – from serenity to festivity

The hall, for 440 people, is sited between the main school and the outlying science and music departments and the routes to these come within its aura. A wish to preserve a view of York Minster gave reason for not attaching it to the main school. Also it was felt that the hall should be a freestanding building, placed pivotal to the complex of school buildings, as is appropriate to its use. It was also felt that such a cardinal building should be architecturally distinctive, fully modelled and of strong formal quality, analogous to freestanding sculpture in a courtyard

For central seating, space top lit from four sides of a high clerestorey is defined on two sides by the walls that separate the crush hall from the main hall, on the third side by the side wall of the building and on the fourth side by a freestanding screen wall which stands in front of the stage curtains. For focused seating this screen wall is raised out of sight and (if necessary) the clerestorey blacked out. Directional artificial lighting, related to shallow recesses in the ceiling over the stage and at the gallery end, change the whole emphasis of the interior, making it appear more elongated and bringing the stage to prominence. By means of movable sections various arrangements can be made for different types of production, eg conventional stage, stage with forestage, stage with orchestra pit. The hall floor can also be flat or in two steps

The building is of reinforced concrete construction, exposed externally (sawn board shutter). The roof is steelwork and consists of two main trusses spanning from stage wall to the two columns at the rear and two cross trusses cantilevering out to carry edge beams on the long sides. These four trusses form a central 'box' carrying a high level roof, and clerestorey light enters the hall through the trusses. The lower roof, surrounding the 'box', spans off the trusses with an 18in gap between it and the lower structure, over which it hovers like a velarium. Ceilings are of expanded metal and plaster. The roof finish is part proprietory sheet, part copper with copper facings and flashings

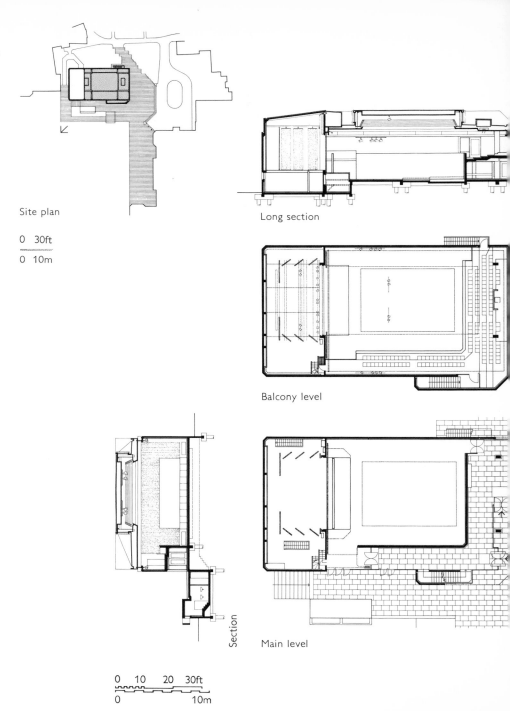

Site plan

0   30ft

0   10m

Long section

Balcony level

Section

Main level

0   10   20   30ft

0   10m

58

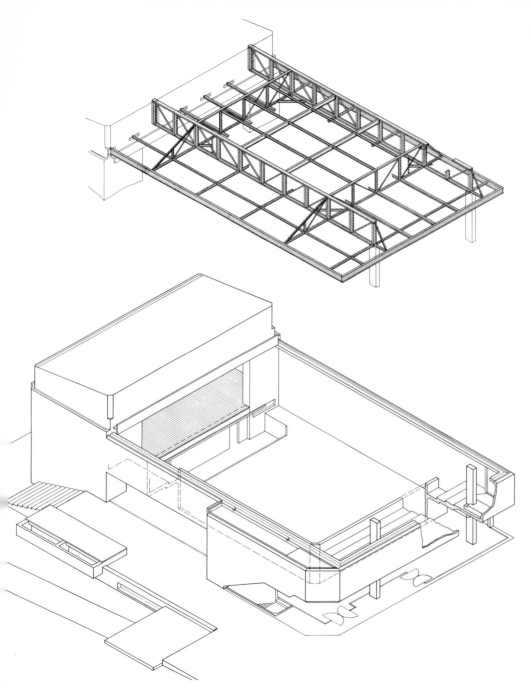

General view from south

Isometric view of concrete structure with steel roof structure projected over

Stage from rear of balcony, arranged for assembly with natural light, screen in position

Stage from rear of balcony, arranged for drama, screen removed, hall blacked out

Hall from west with towers of York Minster beyond

View of hall toward rear from front entrance (on right) of crush hall

Front entrance (as left) and view of crush hall

Main entrance and crush hall at the west corner

Classroom building, Eltham Hill School
ILEA London SE9, 1969

The existing school buildings are of the early 'thirties, in that pleasant brick, tile and timber window manner which was common to LCC buildings of the period. Many similar schools have required internal alteration to provide improved facilities, particularly for science teaching. In this school it was decided to extend laboratory and other accommodation within the old fabric and build to take the overspill and provide further rooms

The new building had to be closely linked to the old without obstructing it or the adjacent field. This consideration, the levels of the site, and a wish for compactness, led to the architectural solution of a pavilion-like building with floors clearly expressed and with modelled profiles. The whole is joined to the old building by a raised walkway. The new rooms thus enjoy good aspect and a fine outlook

The accommodation comprises general and specialized classrooms, two music practice rooms and a 'division' room; also lavatories and stores. The main rooms are planned on three floors with music rooms only on a much smaller fourth floor. The first floor is almost on the level of the terrace to the south of the old building and access is provided at first floor by the raised walkway, as well as ground floor access under it, providing protection in part. The L-shaped hall/stairway is formed between the solid load-bearing structure enclosing service rooms, and the load-bearing back wall of the teaching spaces. The slabs of this are of coffered construction and are supported on a peripheral beam and reinforced concrete columns. The sub-division into two or three classrooms is by means of non-load-bearing but solid walls

The architectural expression comes from the relationship of solid load-bearing core and the framed structure of the open sides of the teaching spaces. The horizontally emphasized spandril walls take the heating service and with set back windows provide secret gutters which take run-off from the building face. The resulting profiling emphasizes the pavilion-like character of the new building against the solidity of the old, while the materials used harmonize in quality and colour

The mansard enclosing the music rooms, the fascias and the column cladding is of copper. Windows are timber with steel opening lights. Cills are of slate and spandril walls of dark facing brick

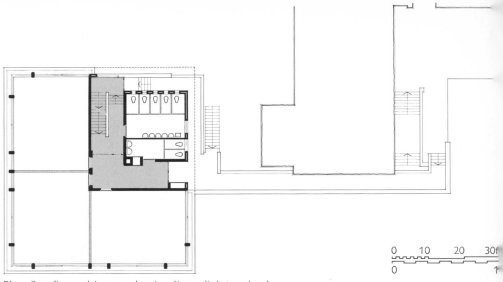

Plan: first floor with upper level walkway link to school

General view from park

64

-east corner, three floors of classrooms, music rooms in mansard

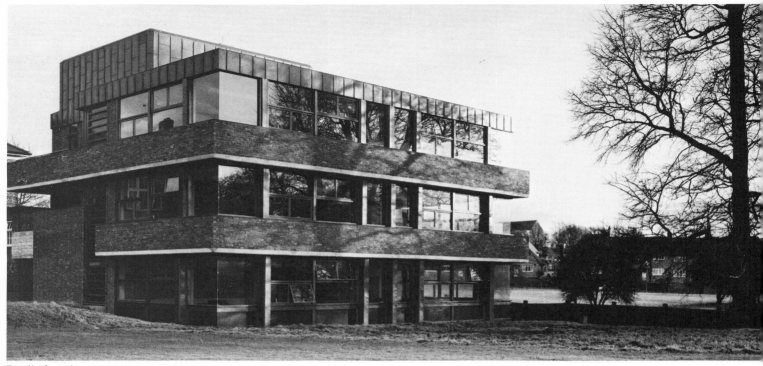

Detail of north-west corner

North-west corner, a classroom interior

Walkway link to school, upper level

Walkway link to school, lower level

40 Berkeley Square, London W1, cinema, studio, reception area 1964

Built as flats in the 1930's, the building was adapted as offices during the war and has been used thus ever since

The clients, having obtained a long lease, implemented a two-stage development plan. The first stage included breakthroughs into the adjoining building at various levels, replanning offices and circulation, provision of social and service areas, meeting rooms, etc., as well as the reconstruction of the principal stairs and replacement of lifts

The second stage was the major building part and included three main spaces. Virtually the whole of the ground floor front was freed to form an extensive entrance and reception area. Two large rooms were built at the basement level of the two light wells of the building, providing a private cinema/presentation room and a separate television studio, while the rest of the basement was reconstructed to provide various film and television facilities

The reception area was planned to one side of the main entrance as an open space in which a free-standing screen provided a 'protected' sitting area and interview bay. The whole area had a low flush ceiling with lighting in random clusters over certain areas. The perimeter of the space had a continuous wide cill echoed by a continuous fascia/cornice over, with concealed lighting. This upper and lower band 'contained' the main wall of the building, with its piers, recesses, various window openings (old and new) and served to define the space in one broad sweep and allowed for display material to be contained within an architectural scheme

The main stairs of the building continued down to a lower foyer from which the cinema/presentation room was entered – a simple rectangular space seating up to hundred and fully equipped for projection and closed circuit TV

Beams spanned from side wall to side wall of the room carrying roof/ceiling slab and angled roof lights which introduced controlled natural light so that the character of the room could be varied. General artificial lighting was incorporated in the roof lights, while the main ceiling featured a large number of miniature lamps. A suspended louvre feature each side concealed further lighting and directional emphasis. The side and rear walls w sub-divided, the upper part faced with acoustic boarding, the lower part projecting beyond the upper face, of blockwork plastered in a sanded finish with rounded arrises and corners. Into t wall, on either side, were set display units, divie into sections and with variable panels providing display backgrounds

The TV working studio was also at basement lev but rising through two storeys, the roof being splayed back on three sides to maintain light ang to ground floor rooms and aluminium faced for reflectance and appearance

Internally, the character was essentially that of a workshop – the room was fully sound insulated ceilings and walls were lined with acoustic mater of different characteristics giving appropriate aco conditions of a very high standard. A ceiling grid provided for fixing lighting and the studio was fu equipped for film and TV work with all necessary supporting facilities in the control gallery and elsewhere. In addition, the studio had its own projection room

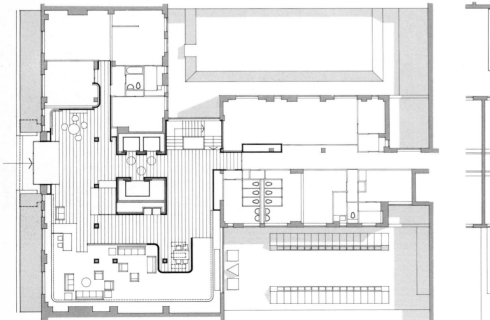

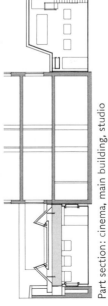

Part section: cinema, main building, studio

0   10   20   30ft

0   10m

Plan: entrance hall and reception. Light wells with studio and cinema roofs

View from bottom of main stair, looking towards reception and waiting area, interview bay

Entrance hall, porter's desk, reception with waiting space beyond. Main doors to the right

Pitcorthie House, Fife 1966

Built on the ruins of an old house to take advantage of the landscaped view to the south with the Burgh of Elie and the sea beyond. The drive-in ends in a generous courtyard formed by reconstructed walls and buildings on the east and north side, a cottage to the west and the house to the south

The main wing, in essence, consists of a core of service rooms surrounded by circulation or living space. The east end is a closed block containing three bedrooms, while the south side, entirely glazed, is a gallery space off which open main bedroom, study and dining room

Entering the dining and general area, with its 'gallery' extension, is a notable experience – the effect of low horizontal interior space, exterior space and view is succeeded by, on turning right up steps into the living room, a secluded and different type of space with ceiling sloping down to windows overlooking terrace and garden to the west

The living room has a generous fireplace, with stack which rises through the highest part to become, externally, a pivotal feature to the design. The roof of the living room carries down beyond the line of the glazing to extend the space visually to the outside. A pillar and beam partly supports the roof, but also suggests sub-division of the space

The interior kitchen gains sunlight from the south clerestorey but there is a broad lift-up shutter so that, if desired, the main outlook can be enjoyed across the dining space. The kitchen is divided by a central worktop with children's dining space beyond linking with the corridor on the north side past a storage wall to the east bedrooms and with a door into the gallery by the master bedroom

The main bedroom and study have sliding doors drawn out from double partitions so they can become self-contained rooms – each with its part of the gallery space. The long end rooms were planned for bunks, with windows facing the east terrace

The bathrooms are centrally planned and lit from the clerestorey

Walls are of stone with some areas of white painted brick. The same materials occur internally together with plaster – all painted white. Floors and ceilings are of timber throughout. The roofs are zinc covered with oak boarded fascias

Site model showing courtyard formed by house, cottage, outbuildings and screened terrace

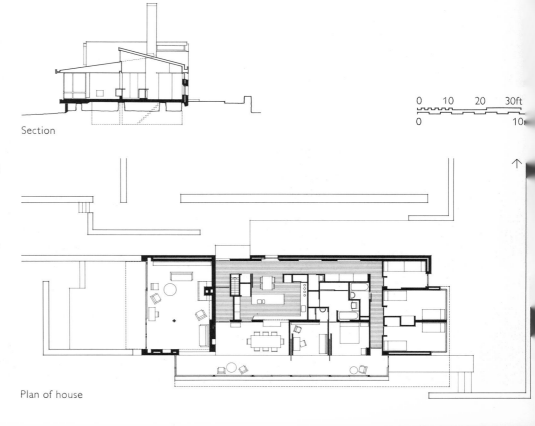

Section

Plan of house

0   10   20   30ft
0   10

South side of house seen from park

West side, living room and terrace

End of living room and junction with gallery

The living room, seen at entrance from gallery, fireplace on right

The gallery with dining space, seen from entrance to living room (left)

Housing, Poplar High Street, GLC London E14, 1966

The form of this building is an answer to a particular problem, a response to an awkward site zoned at 136 persons per acre. The comparatively small number of housing units led to an individual building solution rather than a design for 'housing'

The site lies to the south of Poplar High Street at a gap between the GLC's Galloway Estate and a pre-war Poplar Council scheme, both schemes embodying four to five storey buildings, but otherwise with little affinity. The site opens out southwards, extending to a railway embankment – beyond which are sidings, warehouses and cranes around the docks of the Isle of Dogs

The staggered plan assists the density by the overlapping of flats where the building sets back, it respects light angles, providing excellent outlooks in both directions and prevents a tunnel effect next to the adjacent buildings by the creation of spaces which open out on both sides. Thus the existing buildings have been brought into relation with the new development and by reason of the opening out space, the building is a good neighbour to both schemes, enhancing the setting of each and developing the open effect to the south, out of Poplar High Street

The fall on the site is used to advantage, particularly at the north end. A raised terrace is provided with ramp and step approach from the High Street and the main access to the building is across this nominally ground floor level. However, the fall is such that a lower floor can be provided and here, under the terrace, are the garages, heating chamber, stores and estate workshop, and to the south – three flats with private gardens. Apart from these, the rest of the site is common garden. A small fitted playground has been included and an open drying area (in addition to normal facilities within the building)

The main accommodation consists of seventeen maisonnettes, together with seven old people's two-room or one-room flats. The detail planning is straightforward but at the doubling up the maisonnette plans are modified for lighting from side and end rather than from two ends. The break forward in the side of the building results from this arrangement of the accommodation

The stepped plan incidentally leads to a building

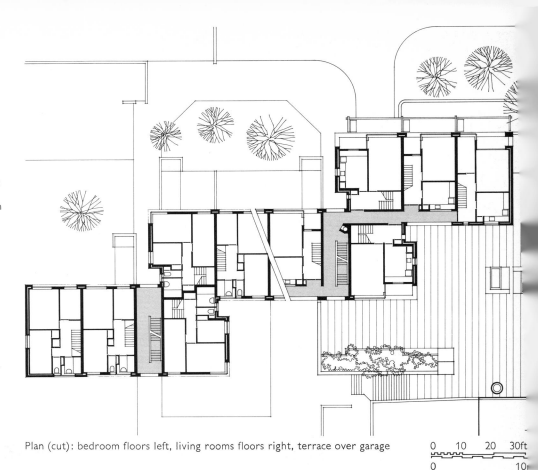

Plan (cut): bedroom floors left, living rooms floors right, terrace over garage

```
0    10    20    30ft
╙────┴────┴────╜
0                10
```

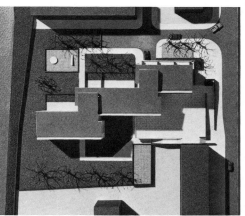

Site model showing adjacent buildings

76

of the west side. Ground floor flats with maisonnettes over

General view of west side showing staggered form of building

teresting overall form which has been
hasized by the arrangement of the one-way
n roof and the projections of the maisonnettes
e breaks. The roofs interlock at the breaks,
re it has been possible to incorporate tank
e without projection – heating mains are taken
ugh the roof space. The roof pitch appears on
nds and break backs, while the long sides are
idered boldly and simply – being divided up by
s vertically (corresponding to cross walls) and
e horizontal bands of concrete every other floor
responding to the living room floors) and which
nd as cantilevers to support the overhang at
breaks in plan. The main units of the façades
espond to the maisonnettes, each being broken
y windows and infill walls between and below
bedroom windows. The brick used throughout
emi-engineering red

End of building to Poplar High Street with ramp from street level to terrace over garage

East side looking towards terrace and High Street beyond

Old people's home, London SW4, 1969

There is room for sixty residents in single, single cubicle and double rooms. Staff flats are also provided

The site falls to the north and kitchen, service, etc., are at a lower level than the main floor. The shape and aspect of the site led to a main wing on the east side with double-banked rooms (east and west aspect) while a second wing at right angles has double rooms on the south side only. These are three-storey but the third wing (west) sets back in plan and is two–storey to open up the space around which the building is planned – a courtyard completed by the link across the south end which provides an ambulatory for residents right round the building at ground floor with widenings at certain points to provide resting places

There are three sitting rooms within the main building and a fourth at the end of the west wing looks over the garden. This has a very different character from the others, one of which faces west while the other two (at either end of the main wing) face east, overlooking the road

The highest point of the building comes where it is most needed architecturally – at the lower end of the site on the road side, marking, with the indent in the main wall, the principal entrance. The projection at the other end marks the independence of the staff flats and their separate entrance

The building is realized in London stock brick, the shallow pitched roofs are aluminium covered and fascias are of oak boards. Sash windows assist the domestic scale which is maintained throughout. Diversity of outlook and aspect give rooms of varied character and interest

Client: London Borough of Lambeth

Section through courtyard, dining room and kitchen wing

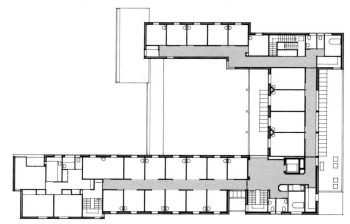

First floor

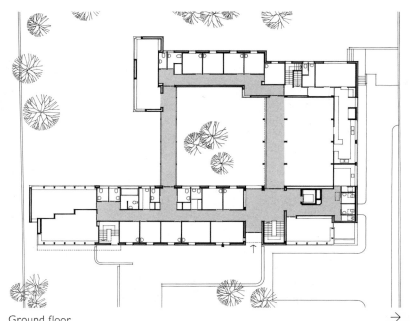

0 10 20 30ft

0 10m

Ground floor

east side seen from Cedars Road, staff accommodation on left, main entrance in recess to right

The garden sitting room, glazed link and courtyard beyond

Detail of garden and link

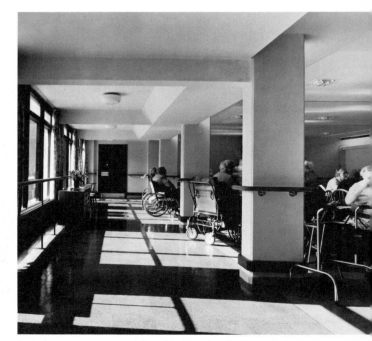

Ambulatory on courtyard (south) side of dining room, clerestorey over

...dren's reception home, London SE15, 1971

...is a short stay centre where children from
...en homes (taken into care) can live while their
...s are assessed and until appropriate fostering
...be arranged for them

...e is little precedent for this building type which
...ires many comparatively small rooms for diverse
...ities as well as the residential needs of about
...y children and a staff of about fifteen

...he first floor the residential side consists of
...dren's rooms (single to 5-bed spaces) integrated
...houseparents' rooms, a wing of three staff
...with independent access and other staff bed-
...ng rooms, sick bays, medical room, etc. On the
...nd floor, a dining room for the whole house
...the necessary service accommodation. For work
...olay, two classrooms, games, hobbies, TV and
...t rooms are provided. A babies' wing, again
...houseparents' rooms. An administrative wing
...offices and interview rooms, etc.

...he first floor, the children's / houseparents'
...ms are in three groups which decided the basic
...e wing plan about a stair hall. The main entrance
...the centre of the fourth wing to the south
...has its own hall with the administration group
...the babies' group on opposite sides and a door
...ne main hall – which increases in width from the
...ance to the space around the projecting foot
...e pivotal stairs. Although the main ground
...rooms (classrooms/recreation on one side,
...ng room on the other) open off it, the hall has
...character of a place rather than a street – some-
...re to linger – analogous to the stair hall of a
...try house. This gave the key to the character
...e building

...ough of some size, with many elements combined
...propriate relationships, the form is broken
...o that from any aspect it appears as a modest
...storey building, near to what might have been
...deal – a converted large house in the country

...t: London Borough of Southwark

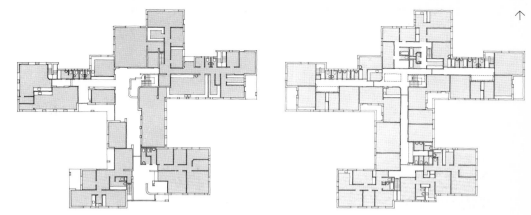

Schematic ground and first floor plans

0   30ft

0   10m

Site model

East side: staff residential over administration, court to dining room, end of service wing, a houseparent's balcony over

Main stair, with lower landing projecting into hall

First floor, landing and clerestoreys

West side: classrooms, social rooms, babies' rooms. Houseparent's and children's rooms on first floor

Riyadh Conference Centre and hotel

This complex is the outcome of a limited competition organized by the International Union of Architects for the Saudi Arabian Government. The competition design was revised and developed and received the approval of His Majesty King Feisal in 1967. The contractors are Cogeco Spa (Italy), the contract sum being SR 78,000,000, and completion will be in 1973. The scheme consists of two closely related but architecturally differentiated buildings: a conference centre and an hotel, as well as a mosque and three villas

The conference centre 'is intended for national and international meetings and seminars and will in time become a cultural focus for the city of Riyadh'. It comprises a hall with seating for 1400 with many technical facilities, three meeting rooms for 150 each, two small meeting rooms, together with exhibition and refreshment areas at different levels and the necessary administration and service spaces. A special VIP entrance and a VIP reception area complete the main accommodation. A large porte cochere breaks forward from the main front of the building and there is a link to the hotel

The brief called for a first-class hotel on generous lines with 200 rooms, guest reception areas and lounges, dining for 300, two private dining rooms and full service accommodation. The approach to the hotel is via a curved, ramped roadway (with covered car parking) leading to the main entrance. The service entrance is between the two buildings behind the link and the central plant room is in the same area. Additional villas, a banquet room and a swimming pool are currently being planned

The conference centre (about 25,000m²) is characterized by a formal, regular system of structure, providing large, free, internal, sun-protected spaces with the auditorium/hall at the heart and other elements grouped around. The hotel (about 16,000m²) is characterized by the accretion of carefully oriented individual units (room, bathroom, patio) about two internal hall spaces. There is, therefore, a contrast between the conference centre, geometrically placed on the site – as a temple – and spatially generous for assembly and interchange, and the more irregular form of the hotel that grows out of the site – like a residential hill

The hall of the conference centre is placed within extensive surrounding foyer spaces planned on three levels. These are:

1. An entrance area opposite the porte cochere which opens into a general foyer and exhibition space the full length of one side of the building – all at the main level

2. An upper level, reached by broad short flights of steps from the general foyer. From this upper foyer a wide group of doorways leads into the middle of the hall – a transition that is a major architectural experience and one which enables participants to come together naturally before and after assembly. This level extends beyond the hall to serve as foyer to the range of meeting rooms

3. A lower level, reached by broad short flights of steps from the main level or by direct stairs from the upper level. This area is a general space – which can be used for exhibitions related to the general foyer, as well as a refreshment area. Off this level are the principal toilets and service areas. The VIP reception is an upper floor forming the ceiling to the offices below (still within the main foyer volume)

The 'hallspace' is square and covered by a space frame steel roof (52m overall) supported on the four diagonally placed corner columns, 39m apart. The hall itself is set within this space and the enclosing walls rise to within 1m of the main ceiling, the gap being filled with heavy glazing. Thus there is effective spatial connection between the inside and outside of the hall through the overriding ceiling, which allows some natural light into the heart of the foyer as well as into the hall. For cinema, blackout blinds are provided integral with the glazing between foyer and hall. In order to provide a calm room, the hall ceiling has been considered as a level but modelled plane (not a sloping plane focussing on to the stage as in a theatre or cinema). It is not a separate element but enmeshes with the structure – consisting of plastered coffers shaped into the pyramids of the steelwork. A number of the coffers contain 'spiders' which carry lighting in their four cross arms and the air distribution grilles in the centre. In the space between the coffered ceiling and the roof slab, conditioned air will be distributed through ducting and there is access to all parts for servicing

Some factors influencing the design of the hotel were:

1. A desire to avoid the faceless pattern of the 'international hotel' and to create an indigenous building of unique character

2. To arrange bedrooms protected from the sun and with maximum privacy, at the same time provid[ing] generous approaches, lounges and other commo[n] space – and the maximum separation of service a[nd] and access

3. To bring guests arriving by car straight to the entrance and to have a large percentage of priva[te] rooms situated with easy reach

All bedrooms face on to private patios, which themselves face away from the sun. The M-form arises from this arrangement and as a result ther[e] are no internal corridors – bedrooms are entere[d] off galleries which overlook the covered courtyar[d] formed within the arms of the bedroom wings. The entrance foyer connects the two courts that r[un] up through the full height of the building, which contains various amenities. The larger court, slightly higher than entrance level, contains the residents' principal lounge, placed to take advantage of the open space of the court and the view to the rear of the main court, where there i[s] an internal garden. In the smaller court, at entran[ce] level, is another lounge which is screened and wil[l] be used for private parties, etc.

These spaces within courts, with their galleries at different levels, are the characteristic feature o[f] the hotel. They are equivalent to outside space, closed, sun-shielded, restful intermediate zones between private rooms and the outside, providing the luxury of architectural space in the 'grand hote[l] tradition, rarely found in a modern hotel

The administrative offices are placed next to the lounge, with easy access from the foyer, but privat[e.] Near the entrance doors is the stair down to the restaurant and adjacent is a walkway which extend[s] as the link between the hotel and conference centr[e.] Either side of this, at the hotel end, space has been provided for small shops as well as the 'coffee shop', opening onto first floor terraces overlooking the extensive evening terraces at restaurant level belo[w]

Model from east. Hotel on right, conference centre beyond, villas and site of mosque in foreground

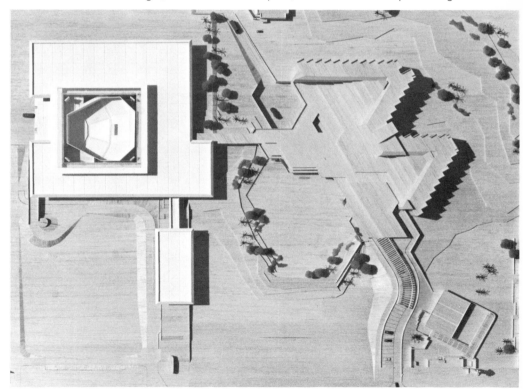

Plan view. Conference centre left (auditorium roof removed) with porte cochere extending to road (bottom), hotel right, mosque bottom right

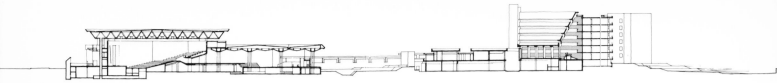

Section: conference centre (auditorium, foyer), link, hotel (reception, restaurant below, lounge, court with galleries, bedrooms)

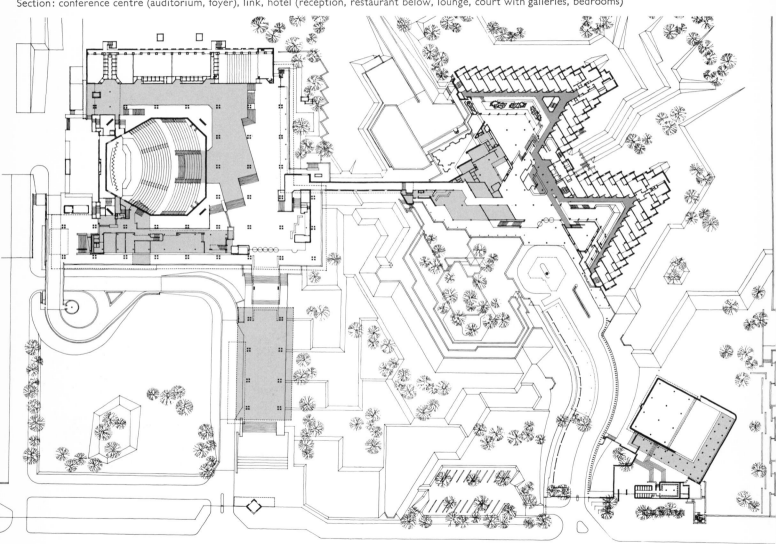

General plan. Left, top to bottom: meeting rooms, upper and general foyers, auditorium, administration, entrance, VIP arrival and ramp, porte cochere, road. Right, top to bottom: service entrance, plant room, etc., bedroom wings with large and small courts, entrance foyer and reception, link to conference centre, evening terrace, arrival area, ramp to road with parking. Mosque. Villas extreme right

rly sketch 'temple and residential hill'

Residents' lounge and principal courtyard of hotel, overlooked by bedroom access galleries

Auditorium model, view toward stage arranged for conference

Auditorium under construction, view toward entrance. One of the four roof columns seen on left

Bedroom galleries, sloping roof over court

Hotel seen from link between porte cochere and conference centre

Conference centre foyer. Exhibition level with stairs to upper foyer leading into auditorium and at far end to meeting rooms. Stairs on left to lower foyer extending under whole area of upper foyer

Conference centre: exhibition area side. Auditorium roof under construction, corner of hotel on left

Model of mosque. Entrance from road with entrance area descending to main courtyard which gives onto the enclosed area of mosque

ed way to villas and courtyard formed by mosque walls

Mosque interior – brown concrete structure, white free-standing walls

Minaret: white concrete with oak super-structure

Acknowledgements

Over twenty years there are many who must be thanked for their collaboration, especially the following:

Architects and designers

John Barrow
James Bruges
Michael Burrell
Michael Collings
Colin Dollimore (associate)
David Greenwood
Martin Grierson
Roger Monson
Ronald Paxton (associate)
Innis Read
Drew Stevenson
David Stewart
Katharine Tilbury

For Riyadh

Colin Dollimore, project architect, hotel
Ronald Paxton, project architect, conference centre
Eli Clarke
Richard Clarke (special responsibility for mosque and villas, now resident architect)
Roger Coombs
Rolf Derenbach
David Greenwood
Andrew Hauser
Edward Hughes
Susan Jackson
Terence Jordan
Britte Kjeldegaard
Siegfried Kendel
Thomas Krayer
Elizabeth Love
Anthony Mobbs
Roger Myers
Stuart Page
John Scorah
Mary Scott
Drew Stevenson

Consulting engineers

Structural:
Kenchington, Little and Partners
Jenkins and Potter
Ove Arup and Partners

Structural, Riyadh:
Ove Arup and Partners, Structures III
Riyadh group led by Ian Liddell
Senior resident engineer representing Trevor Dannatt/Ove Arup and Partners, Peter Woodward
Assistant resident engineer, Nicholas Madinaveitia

Services, Riyadh:
Dale and Ewbank

Quantity surveyors

Monk and Dunstone
Franklin and Andrews
Widnell and Trollope (Riyadh)

Contractors

F. W. Clifford Ltd:
Pollock, Lund Humphries London, 40 Berkeley Square
William Mills and Sons:
Congregational church and chapel
Leslie Bilsby Ltd/ Prowting:
Dobbs House
G. B. Brudenell Ltd:
Laslett House
Field Davis Ltd:
Plante House
L. H. Beal and Sons Ltd:
Needler Hall, Bootham
Coulson & Son Ltd:
Trinity Hall
Johnson and Bailey Ltd:
Vaughan, Leicester library
J. C. Kellett & Son Ltd:
Council chamber
R. Durtnell and Son Ltd:
Eltham Hill
Alex Fraser Ltd:
House in Fife
J. and J. Dean (Contracts) Ltd:
Poplar
W. J. Simms Son and Cooke Ltd:
Old people's home, SW
F. C. Steele and Partners Ltd:
Children's reception home
Cogeco Spa, Rome:
Riyadh

The book

Colin Forbes
Christine Cope
Roger Coombs, who did the drawings

Photographers

John Dewar
Frank Donaldson
Edgar Hyman
Mann Brothers
Colin Westwood

and

Ted Happold
Susan Kirkeby
John Shaw